Mridula Baljekar's

South-east Asian Curry Cookbook

Mridula Baljekar's
South-east Asian
Curry Cookbook

Over 50 deliciously fresh and fragrant curries from Thailand,
Burma, Vietnam, Indonesia, Malaysia and the Philippines

southwater

This edition is published by Southwater, an imprint of Anness Publishing Ltd, Hermes House,
88–89 Blackfriars Road, London SE1 8HA; tel. 020 7401 2077; fax 020 7633 9499

www.southwaterbooks.com; www.annesspublishing.com

If you like the images in this book and would like to investigate using them for publishing, promotions or advertising, please visit
our website www.practicalpictures.com for more information.

UK agent: The Manning Partnership Ltd; tel. 01225 478444; fax 01225 478440; sales@manning-partnership.co.uk
UK distributor: Grantham Book Services Ltd; tel. 01476 541080; fax 01476 541061; orders@gbs.tbs-ltd.co.uk
North American agent/distributor: National Book Network; tel. 301 459 3366; fax 301 429 5746; www.nbnbooks.com
Australian agent/distributor: Pan Macmillan Australia; tel. 1300 135 113; fax 1300 135 103; customer.service@macmillan.com.au
New Zealand agent/distributor: David Bateman Ltd; tel. (09) 415 7664; fax (09) 415 8892

Publisher: Joanna Lorenz
Managing Editor: Judith Simons
Project Editor: Sarah Ainley
Designer: Nigel Partridge
Reference section: Mridula Baljekar and Sallie Morris
Recipes: Mridula Baljekar, Kit Chan, Rafi Fernandez, Deh-Ta Hsiung, Shehzad Husain,
Christine Ingram, Manisha Kanani, Sally Mansfield, Sallie Morris and Jennie Shapter
Photography: Edward Allwright, David Armstrong, Nicki Dowey, Amanda Heywood, Ferguson Hill,
Janine Hosegood, David Jordan, David King, Patrick McLeavey and Sam Stowell
Jacket Photography: Nicki Dowey
Production Controller: Claire Rae

ETHICAL TRADING POLICY
Because of our ongoing ecological investment programme, you, as our customer, can have the pleasure and reassurance of
knowing that a tree is being cultivated on your behalf to naturally replace the materials used to make the book you are holding.
For further information about this scheme, go to www.annesspublishing.com/trees

Front cover shows a variation of Red Chicken Curry, for recipe see page 38

Previously published as part of a larger volume, *Curry*.

NOTES
Bracketed terms are intended for American readers. For all recipes, quantities are given in both metric and imperial measures
and, where appropriate, measures are also given in standard cups and spoons. Follow one set, but not a mixture,
because they are not interchangeable.
Standard spoon and cup measures are level. 1 tsp = 5ml, 1 tbsp = 15ml, 1 cup = 250ml/8fl oz
Australian standard tablespoons are 20ml. Australian readers should use 3 tsp in place of 1 tbsp for measuring small quantities
of gelatine, flour, salt, etc.
Medium (US large) eggs are used unless otherwise stated.

CONTENTS

INTRODUCTION

Burma, Thailand, Vietnam, Malaysia, Indonesia and the Philippines are the principal countries in the region known as South-east Asia. This corner of the Asian continent is steeped in ancient tradition and heritage, and has a chequered history of new lands discovered, empires built and destroyed, valuable allies and dangerous enemies. Central to the dramas that have unfolded are the exotic spices that have grown here for centuries. It is the carefully prepared blends of these spices that provide the mouthwatering flavours and aromas of curries.

Below: This Filipino meat soup, known as Puchero, has its origins in Spanish cookery.

South-east Asia occupies an important place in the history of the spice trade. The use of premium quality spices in these sun-drenched, monsoon-fed lands was an established way of life long before traders, among them Arabs, English, Dutch, Portuguese and Spanish, came to the area, lured by the valuable exotic spices.

Spectacular geography, fascinating ancient customs, and glorious foods all continue to draw foreigners to these magical lands. From Burma's border with China in the north to the beaches of Indonesia's paradise islands in the south, this corner of the world is diverse in every respect.

Above: The fried rice dish Nasi Goreng is a good way to use up leftover rice and meat.

Just as much as the breathtakingly beautiful scenery, culinary traditions have also been influenced by geographical and climatic conditions. With vast distances to be travelled, and no means of transporting fresh produce efficiently, cook's have made the best use of the ingredients available locally.

Besides offering fabulous flavours, South-east Asian cooking is extremely healthy. The emphasis is firmly on freshness, with a wide range of meats, fish and shellfish, vegetables and salads. Meat and fish are served in small quantities, surrounded by inviting little side dishes, such as salads and sambals, flavoured with fresh herbs, chillies and soy sauce, and used as seasonings. Rice or noodles form the staple diet in South-east Asia. Many of the ingredients used in these dishes are known for their medicinal properties. For example, there is strong evidence that garlic and fresh root ginger, two of the most essential ingredients in curries,

Right: This Indonesian squid dish uses spices introduced by Indian and Arab traders.

contain properties that can help to combat heart diseases and stomach ulcers respectively.

The Indian commercial community, who emigrated to South-east Asia, added their own identity to local cuisines and customs, and this has helped to merge culinary practices. The Indian influence is strongest in Malaysia, while the cuisines of Vietnam and the islands of the Philippines have profound French and Spanish legacies. Only Thailand has remained free from colonial rule.

The striking resemblance in many of the cooking and serving styles of Indian and South-east Asian curries is reflected in the ingredients used. The exquisite flavour of cardamom pods, the warmth of cumin, the sweet, mellow taste of fresh coriander, the woody aroma of ginger and fiery chillies are classic flavours. Coconut-based curries from south India resemble those of South-east Asia in taste and aroma.

Culinary skills and expertise from around the world have been developed in South-east Asia, and the best of the resulting dishes are featured in this wonderful collection. The aim of this volume is to offer traditional South-east Asian curry recipes with authentic flavours and uncomplicated preparation and cooking methods. I hope it will encourage even novice cooks to get to know the delights of cooking hot and spicy curries.

MRIDULA BALJEKAR

Right: Piquant sambals are served with rice, curries, salads and vegetable side dishes.

SOUTH-EAST
ASIA

Some of the world's most exciting cuisines

are found in the south-eastern corner of Asia.

Throughout the region, in Burma, Thailand and

Vietnam, Malaysia and the islands of Indonesia

and the Philippines, each country has its own

traditional cooking style, yet all share a passion for

fragrant, flavoursome dishes, with an emphasis

on using only the freshest of ingredients.

CULTURE and CUISINE

South-east Asian food is a joy to the senses, combining the refreshing aroma of lemon grass and kaffir lime leaves with the pungency of brilliant red chillies and the magical flavours of coconut milk and fresh basil. The curries of the region follow this tradition for flavourings, and they are very different from their Indian counterparts: lemon grass and kaffir lime leaves are rarely used in the Indian subcontinent. Furthermore, Indian curries are traditionally slow-cooked for a rich and creamy taste, while South-east Asian dishes are famously quick and easy to prepare.

The popularity of South-east Asian foods is now firmly established in the West and it continues to grow. Supermarkets and greengrocers have started selling many of the more exotic ingredients from the area: lemon grass, Thai chillies and galangal are all readily available, as are coconut and the milk

Below: A simple South-east Asian meal might include rice and noodles, eaten with hot relishes and deep-fried onions.

and cream extracted from it. The appeal of South-east Asian food is obvious: it is full of flavour, always colourful and healthy, with an emphasis on serving the freshest possible foods.

Climate and geography
The area known as South-east Asia starts with Burma near the north-eastern border of India and incorporates Thailand, Cambodia and Vietnam, as well as Malaysia and Singapore in the South China Sea. It includes Indonesia, which, with its 13,000 islands, is the largest archipelago in the world. To the east lies Borneo and, beyond that, the Philippines. The whole area has been referred to as Farther India by European scholars, because of its position at the far side of the Ganges.

For such a vast area, there is surprisingly little temperature variation: a result of the region's location in the tropical belt along the Equator. The countries have long stretches of coastline, and all have their own distinctive geographical and climatic

conditions. Irrigated rice fields co-exist with marshlands; majestic snow-capped mountains stand in sharp contrast to lush green rainforests.

Local resources
Such varied conditions have naturally given rise to a wide range of crops, resulting in cuisines that are distinctly different from one country to another. All of the countries enjoy the plentiful fish and shellfish provided by their seas and rivers, and these have become part of the daily diet everywhere. Another common element is rice, the staple food of the whole of Asia. Rice is grown in abundance, as the warm, moist tropical climate provides ideal growing conditions. Noodles also form an important part of the Asian diet, and are usually cooked with other ingredients as part of a dish, rather than served on the side as an accompaniment. Root crops, such as yam and cassava, are cooked in a variety of ways, and are sometimes used as a staple instead of rice and noodles.

Outside influences
The influence of religion on food is pronounced across the whole of Asia, but it is especially apparent in the South-east, where there is a wide variety of beliefs, including Hinduism, Buddhism, Islam and Christianity, along with a range of cultural practices, both indigenous and imposed. Indeed, foreign settlers, traders and invaders have had a significant impact on the cuisine of most countries in the area, one exception being Thailand, which has never been invaded or colonized.

In the 16th century, the Portuguese were among the first European powers to exploit the area, although colonization did not begin until much later. The initial appeal of South-east Asia for Europeans was its spices: the area is noted for the Spice Islands, where Arab traders had long been active. Nutmeg and peppercorns were especially highly prized, and European trading began in these commodities. The Dutch, French, British, Spanish and North Americans colonized the area and had an impact on its cuisine, which is still noticeable today.

REGIONAL DIVERSITY

The food culture of South-east Asia varies widely across the region, with each country following its own long-standing traditions for spice blends, flavourings and cooking styles. However, there are also many similarities, largely because of the trade in ingredients, the influences of climate, geography and religion, and of powerful neighbouring countries, such as China.

Thailand

Between Burma and Vietnam lies Thailand, the only country in South-east Asia that has never been colonized by European powers. The word *thai* means free, and the people of Thailand are proud of their independence. In terms of size, Thailand is roughly equal to Burma, but smaller than both India and China. It is divided into five regions, each with its own distinctive geography and culture.

Bangkok, the capital of Thailand, is popularly known as the Venice of the East, because the city is built around

Below: The South-east Asian region covers a multitude of countries, all quite individual.

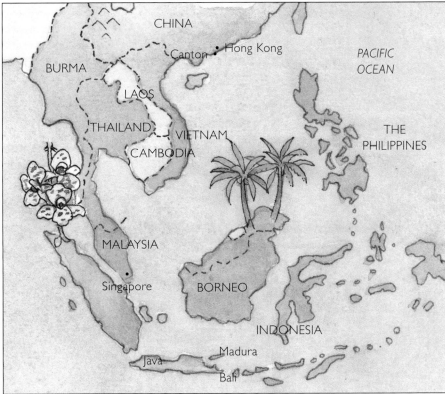

Above: A Thai hod market, so named because farmers display their produce in open baskets, which they carry to market on the ends of long poles, known as hods.

extensive inland waterways, and the majority of the city's population lives along the numerous canals. The floating markets are the workplace of a vast number of people, who sell fruits and vegetables, chillies, fresh fish and a wealth of other exotic ingredients. Thailand is renowned for its excellence in the art of fruit and vegetable carving, and an enjoyable day can be spent watching the various demonstrations on the streets of Bangkok.

Buddhism is the religion of Thailand, although most people seem to have a fairly liberal attitude to Buddhist law, and Thai cuisine includes an extensive range of meat-based recipes. It is fish, shellfish and vegetables, however, that constitute the main part of the Thai diet. Salads are central to a Thai meal, and there are many varieties made, some of which use exotic fruits such as mangoes, pineapple and papaya, as well as raw vegetables. A small quantity of shredded meat, such as pork, is sometimes added, perhaps with perhaps a few prawns (shrimp). Thai salad dressings are a delicious blend of fish sauce, brown sugar and lime juice.

The particular climate conditions and geographical position of Thailand have given rise to regional variations in the nation's cuisine. In southern Thailand, the Gulf of Thailand and the Andaman Sea provide a wealth of fish and shellfish. Dishes based on these ingredients are popular throughout the country, but are particularly important in the south. In the north, where the climate is slightly cooler, fruits such as lychees are grown in abundance. Chicken, fish and glutinous rice are eaten in the north-east.

Coconut plays a very important role in Thai cooking. Coconut milk, flavoured with ginger, lemon grass, pungent local chillies and basil leaves, forms the basis of most Thai curries. Many desserts are also made using coconut milk and palm sugar. Whatever the dish, there is always a fine balance and complexity of flavour, texture and colour. Thai people regard food as a celebration, and it is considered bad luck to eat alone.

Burma

Colonized by the British in the late 19th century, Burma finally gained its independence in 1948, after a politically turbulent period, one year after the end of British rule in India. The country was officially renamed Myanmar in 1989. The national religion of Burma is Buddhism, which, like Hinduism, forbids

Below: The lively and colourful floating markets on the waterways of Burma sell supplies of fresh fish, fruits and vegetables.

the taking of another life for reasons of personal gratification. Although strict followers observe this rule, in practice most people eat a fair amount of meat, and fish is even more popular: Mohingha (Burmese Fish Stew) is flavoured with Indian spices, and is almost the national dish. Burmese food has noticeable Indian and Chinese influences. Spices from India are often sold in the local street markets, although the country's cuisine generally has more subtle flavours than its Indian counterpart. Rice is the staple food, but noodles, a Chinese contribution, are also very popular. The use of groundnut (peanut) oil and coconut suggests an Indian influence, whereas sesame oil, which is also used as a cooking medium, is a distinctly Chinese ingredient.

Vietnam

Lying virtually next door to Thailand, Vietnam has a cuisine that is in a class of its own. The country was ruled by the French for nearly 80 years, and a French culinary influence can still be detected. The most prominent influence, however, is that of the Chinese, who occupied Vietnam for nearly a thousand years.

Vietnamese food is light and delicate, and the use of fat is limited. Generally speaking, the Vietnamese prefer spicy food, with a well-balanced flavour and a clean taste. Rice and noodles are once again the staples, as in other South-east Asian countries. Plenty of fresh fruit and vegetables are consumed, along with small quantities of meat, and fish and shellfish feature high on the menus.

Malaysia

Bordering Thailand in the north and Indonesia in the south, Malaysia is a lush, tropical land, with widely varying landscapes. It has a genuine diversity of races and cultures, and this is reflected in the country's varied cuisine. Navigation is easy throughout this area, and people have long been able to exchange cooking styles and ingredients with neighbouring countries.

The culinary heritage of Malaysia reaches back for at least six centuries, when the country began to attract

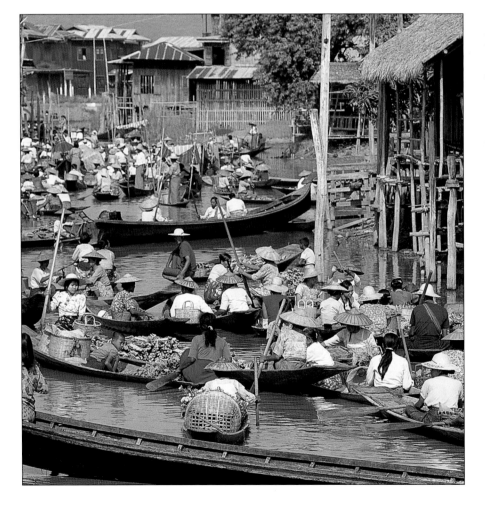

between southern Indian and Malaysian cooking, with only minor differences, such as the use of lime leaves in Malaysian cooking and curry leaves in south Indian.

The tremendous variety in Malaysian cuisine is also partly a result of the range of religious beliefs within the country. For example, no pork is eaten among the Muslim community, although pork is a particular favourite of the Chinese. The Hindus from India will not eat beef, whereas the local Malay population has excellent beef-based recipes. Dishes such as rendang and sambal, which suggest an Indonesian influence, exist side by side with biryanis and samosas, which are unmistakably Indian. The Malaysian dessert *gula melaka* is a superb local creation, which is made with sago, enriched with thick coconut milk and sweetened with palm sugar with a touch of spices.

Indonesia

Comprising 13,000 islands spread along the Indian Ocean, Indonesia is a lush, green fertile land with steamy tropical heat and snow-capped mountain peaks.

For over two thousand years, waves of foreign traders and merchants entered the islands, and Hindu, Muslim

traders and travellers from far-flung places. India and Arabia were the first to exploit the country for its precious goods, followed by the Chinese and Portuguese. Trading began in such commodities as raw silk, brocades, fine silver and pearls, which were exchanged for peppercorns (known as black gold in those days), cloves, nutmeg and mace. Chinese princesses were sent by the emperor as gifts for the Malay sultan. Many Chinese men came to Malaysia to find work, married local women and settled in the country. This started a culture of Chinese food in Malaysia, to which the local people added their own touch. A new style of cuisine was thus created, which had Chinese influences, but flavours that were essentially local.

Above: A street stall in Singapore. One of the strongest influences on Malay cuisine has come from Chinese migrant workers.

Right: A typical Indonesian farmhouse on the island of Java. Green vegetables grow well in this lush tropical climate.

Southern India has also had an impact on Malaysian cooking, as Indian workers from the south were hired to work in the rubber plantations in Malacca. There are striking resemblances evident

on the cuisine of the country. The most significant influences on eating habits undoubtably came from the Hindus and Muslims, and the Chinese.

In no other South-east Asian country does rice play such a major role as in Indonesia. It is eaten twice a day with numerous types of curry. On the island of Bali, Hindus eat rice with fish curries, Muslims eat it with beef and chicken, and the Chinese eat it with almost any meat, including duck. The famous Indonesian style of serving a meal, known as *nasi gerai* (loosely translated as the rice table), was even popular with the Dutch. *Nasi* means rice and *gerar* refers to the endless variety of other dishes served with it. Nasi Goreng (fried rice) is one of the best-known dishes, along with Gado Gado, a cooked vegetable salad with a delicious peanut dressing. Beef Rendang, with the pungency of chillies and ginger, the warmth of cumin and the sweet, mellow flavour of coconut milk, is one of Indonesia's most enduring dishes.

The Philippines

Like that of its neighbours, Filipino cooking is a harmonious blend of the cuisine of many countries and cultures. There are notable similarities with other South-east Asian countries, in terms of the way that ingredients are grown, prepared and cooked.

The original Filipinos are believed to have been of Malayo-Polynesian origin, but the age of discovery and exploitation brought traders from many neighbouring countries, including China, Malaysia, Japan and Indonesia. However, the strongest influence came from the Spanish, who arrived in the 16th century. They ruled the country for nearly 400 years, and during that time they established Christianity, making the Philippines the only Asian country with the Christian faith. Filipinos love both siestas and fiestas, which are both legacies from the Spanish. Dishes such as Bombonese Arroz (rice fritters), Arroz Caldo (rice with chicken) and Puchero (a mixed meat soup) are among the more popular Spanish-influenced dishes still eaten

and Buddhist kingdoms have all been established and destroyed. The Hindus in the 1st century, and the Buddhists in the 8th, established a vegetarian ethos, based on their own strict religious beliefs. Arab traders introduced Islam in the 15th century, and even today the Muslim community in Indonesia does not eat pork. Along with the Arabs, the Indians and Chinese were the first traders to visit Indonesia, lured by its spices, and by nutmeg, mace and cloves, in particular. Arab traders took shiploads of these spices into Europe and sold them at highly inflated prices.

The Europeans soon saw the benefit of eliminating the middle man, and the Portuguese, Dutch, English and Spanish all began sailing to Indonesia themselves, referring to the islands as the Spice

Above: Local fishermen leave freshly caught mackerel to dry in the hot midday sun on the beaches of Bali, Indonesia.

Islands of the East. The Portuguese and British set up trading posts, but the Dutch eventually colonized Indonesia, and they stayed for 250 years, until the country gained independence in 1945. Throughout the period of Dutch rule, Chinese migrants, traders and workers continued to add their own distinctive traditions to the already rich tapestry of Indonesian culture.

With such diverse cultural influences, Indonesian cuisine emerged as one of the most varied and interesting in the whole of South-east Asia. Yet, although Indonesia was a Dutch colony, the Dutch themselves have had very little impact

Above: *Rice is the principal crop grown on the intricately terraced fields in the Luzon region of the Philippines. These terraces will provide employment for all inhabitants of the immediate area.*

today. Before the arrival of the Spanish, the Americans came to the area, and together these two influences helped to make Filipino cuisine a harmonious blend of Eastern and Western styles.

Chinese influence was also strong in the area, and this is clearly evident from the endless variety of noodle-based dishes. Pansit Guisado (Noodles with Chicken, Prawns and Ham) is just one of a number of popular Chinese-inspired dishes. Rice is the staple food of the Philippines, however, and it is eaten daily with almost every meal, even breakfast. The everyday diet of Filipinos is based on a simple dish of rice, stir-fried with meat, fish and vegetables.

Adobo, a Filipino spicy stew made with pork, chicken or even fish and shellfish, is a real speciality of the islands. The sauce in which the ingredients are cooked is an irresistible blend of flavours, combining the tartness of local palm vinegar with the spiciness of black peppercorns and the unmistakable, pungent flavour of garlic. Although it owes much to Spanish origins, the dish, like so much of Filipino food, has its own distinctive character.

Left: *Fishermen prepare to haul up their nets on the Calamian Islands, in the Philippines. The boat is known as a banca.*

PRINCIPLES of SOUTH-EAST ASIAN COOKING

Food takes centre stage in the daily life of most people in South-east Asian. It is a well-known fact that food brings people together, and nowhere is this more apparent than across the Asian region. Food is one of life's greatest pleasures, and sharing it with family and friends is fundamental to the cultures of these countries. Quite simply, they live to eat.

All over South-east Asia, food is prepared with great attention to detail, using only the freshest ingredients. Dishes are healthy and easy to cook, with enough visual appeal to tempt anyone. Until fairly recently, recipes were not written down, but were handed down from generation to generation. The lack of written recipes has encouraged cooks to use their imagination when creating dishes, to experiment with flavours, while keeping to the principles of their local cooking styles and techniques.

Spices and aromatics

South-east Asian cooks are skilled in the art of combining spices, which they use to add taste, colour and aroma.

The essential spices of South-east Asia are coriander, cumin, turmeric, chilli and peppercorns, and although the same spices are used in India, the curries of South-east Asia are quite different, with a milder heat and more subtle flavours.

As in India, South-east Asian cuisine also makes use of whole spices, which are removed at the end of cooking. These include cinnamon, cloves and cardamom pods, and they are especially popular in Malaysia, where the influence of Indian cuisine is most strongly felt.

Adding flavour

Spice blends are usually combined with coconut milk, the most commonly used ingredient, and other hallmark ingredients, such as lemon grass and kaffir lime leaves. Most South-east Asian curries have a distinctive tangy taste, which comes from tamarind, the souring agent that is characteristic of all Asian cooking. Lime juice and vinegar are also used, and these add a refreshing tartness to curries, while the addition of soy sauce, fish sauce or shrimp paste gives that particular depth and pungent flavour that is so distinctive to South-east Asian cuisine. Among the fresh ingredients used as flavouring agents are shallots, galangal, ginger, garlic and chilli, as well as an array of fresh herbs, especially coriander (cilantro), mint and basil.

Below: Each country in South-east Asia has its own individual cooking style, but the essential approach to eating is the same: food is always fresh, full of flavour and carefully prepared and presented.

PREPARING a SOUTH-EAST ASIAN CURRY

Despite the many regional variations, South-east Asian curries are prepared following the same basic pattern. The differences in the cuisines can be attributed more to culture, lifestyle and local food resources, than to alternative cooking techniques.

Basic ingredients
The first point to consider when making any curry is what cooking medium to use. Coconut and palm oil are widely used throughout South-east Asia, and people in some countries, such as Thailand and the Philippines, use lard. To avoid consuming too much saturated fat, use a lighter cooking oil, such as vegetable oil or sunflower oil.

In South-east Asia, stock is more frequently used than water when making curries. This is probably because meat and poultry are cut into small pieces and are generally cooked off the bone. Stock adds an extra depth of flavour.

For thickening sauces, the common practice is to rely on ingredients such as coconut milk, grated coconut, onions, grated fresh root ginger and crushed garlic. In all curries, colour and pungency are created by the addition of different types of chillies, in varying amounts.

Cooking a curry
The starting point when making a curry is to preheat the oil and fry the onions, which, along with garlic and ginger, are the basic ingredients of all South-east Asian curries. Sometimes the onions are fried until they are crisp before the garlic and ginger are added, while in other dishes they are simply softened. The spices or curry paste are then added and cooked for a short time to eliminate their raw flavour. When the spices are cooked to the right point, the oil begins to separate from the thick spice paste.

By using a wide range of cooking techniques, a variety of flavours can be created from the same basic ingredients: recipes such as Beef Rendang and Thai Mussaman Curry are good examples of this. Although a recipe should initially be used as a guide, it is much more fun to be able to stamp your own personality

Above: *Spices and aromatics can be used in many ways, and different flavours can be created from the same ingredients.*

on to whatever you are cooking. This becomes easier with practice, and, after a while, using spices to prepare delicious South-east Asian curries becomes a work of art. Start to use spices as an artist uses a palette, as you tone and colour the food to your own taste.

Planning and serving
Dishes served at a South-east Asian meal are not categorized into separate courses, but are all brought to the table at the same time. Diners help themselves with many helpings of small quantities.

Rice is the cornerstone of all meals, and is served with one or two vegetable side dishes, relishes (such as different types of sambal), salads and curries. It is customary to serve more than one meat or poultry dish, a vegetable curry and a dry, spiced, stir-fried vegetable dish. A soup is another important part of a South-east Asian meal. Desserts are not generally served, except in Malaysia, where delicious hot and cold rice or sago desserts are cooked in coconut milk, sweetened with palm sugar.

Freezing foods
South-east Asian dishes are prepared very quickly, as meat and vegetables are cut into small pieces so that they can be stir-fried, and they are not marinated before cooking. As time-saving strategies, therefore, chilling and freezing are probably not as important in South-east Asian cuisine as they are to some other types of cooking. However, curries always taste better if they are cooked a day or two in advance. The spices seem to permeate the meat and poultry, and the final flavour is much more mellow.

If you plan to freeze the food you are cooking, the following basic guidelines may be helpful:
• Leave the food slightly underdone.
• Cool the food rapidly. The best way to do this is to tip it into a large tray (a large roasting pan is ideal) and leave it in a cool place.
• Once the food has cooled down, put it into appropriate containers, then label and chill it before finally putting it in the freezer. The food will keep in the freezer for 6–8 months, depending on the star rating of your freezer.
• Food from unplanned freezing, such as leftovers, should not be frozen for longer than 2–3 months.

AROMATICS, SPICES and HERBS

Spices are fresh or dried aromatic parts of plants, including leaves, seeds, bark and roots. Some spices are used for the taste they impart, while others, known as aromatics, are used for aroma. Spices should be added with care: one spice used on its own can completely alter the taste of a dish, and a mixture of spices will affect colour and texture. Fresh and dried herbs also play an important part in the combinations of flavour, colour and aroma and, because herbs require only minimal cooking, they retain an intensity of flavour and fragrance.

The quantities of spices and salt specified in recipes are measured to achieve a balance of flavours. In some cases, however, you may prefer to increase or decrease the quantities according to taste. This is particularly true of fresh chillies and chilli powder: experiment with quantities, adding less than specified, if wished.

Garlic

This is a basic ingredient in much of South-east Asian cooking. Vietnamese cooks use a great deal of garlic, and in Thailand a mixture of crushed garlic, coriander (cilantro) root and pepper is the foundation of many dishes. Garlic is an essential ingredient in Thai curry pastes, and it is used throughout South-east Asia, to flavour oil for frying, partly because of the aromatic flavour it imparts, and also because it cuts down on the oiliness of the finished dish. Raw garlic is used in dips, marinades and dressings, and pickled garlic is used as a pickling spice in relishes and sambals.

MAKING GARLIC OIL

1 Heat 120ml/4fl oz/½ cup vegetable oil in a small pan. Add 30ml/2 tbsp crushed garlic to the pan, and stir it into the oil. Cook gently for about 5 minutes, stirring occasionally.

2 Continue to cook the garlic in the oil until it is pale gold in colour. Do not let it burn or the oil will taste bitter. Allow to cool, then strain into a sterilized jar and use as required.

Ginger

Fresh root ginger has a refreshing scent, reminiscent of citrus, and a pleasant, sharp flavour. Young ginger is tender and mild enough to be stir-fried as a vegetable, while older roots are fibrous and more pungent. Root ginger is now widely available in the West. It is also sold dried and as a paste, but these taste quite different to fresh. Both are used mainly as pickling spices, and Asian cooks do not consider them an acceptable substitute for the fresh root. Ground ginger tastes different again; in South-east Asia its use is limited to mixing with other spices, such as when making curry powder.

Above: Fresh garlic

***Above**: Clockwise from top, fresh ginger, ground ginger and ginger paste*

PREPARING FRESH ROOT GINGER

Fresh root ginger is peeled before use. The thin, tough outer skin is easily scraped or cut away, and the flesh is grated, sliced or chopped.

1 Thinly peel the skin using a sharp knife or vegetable peeler.

2 Grate the peeled root finely.

3 Alternatively, cut the ginger into thin batons, then chop the batons coarsely before adding to the dish.

4 Bruise the root with the flat blade of a knife, if it will be removed from the dish and discarded before serving.

Above: From left, fresh galangal and dried galangal

Lengkuas

A member of the ginger family, lengkuas has a creamy coloured root with rings on the skin, and pink nodules. Fresh lengkuas is prepared and used in the same way as fresh root ginger. Ground lengkuas is also available, although the flavour is no match for the fresh root: use 5ml/1 tsp to replace 2.5cm/1in fresh lengkuas. Galangal can be used as a substitute for lengkuas.

Galangal

This is an essential flavouring agent in South-east Asian cooking, particularly in shellfish and meat dishes. It is often pounded with shallots, garlic and chillies to make a spice paste for dips or curries. In Thailand, slices of galangal are added to soups with shreds of lemon grass and lime leaves, while Vietnamese cooks add it to a peanut and lime sauce used as a dressing for meat and vegetable salads.

Greater galangal has a pine-like aroma and a sharp flavour; lesser galangal is more pungent, and a cross between ginger and black pepper. The rhizome is usually used fresh, but it is also avaaible dried and as a powder, known as laos.

Right: Ground turmeric and fresh turmeric

Turmeric

Although it comes from the ginger family, turmeric has none of the heat associated with fresh root ginger. Referred to as "Indian saffron", it shares saffron's capacity to tint food yellow, but is not as subtle as the more expensive spice. The bright yellow colour is also used as a dye for silks and cottons, including the robes of Buddhist monks. Fresh turmeric imparts a warm, musky flavour and a rich colour to foods. The dried spice has similar properties. Ground turmeric is used in curry powders, and is responsible for the characteristic yellow colour.

PREPARING FRESH CHILLIES

The recipes that call for two or more chillies will be quite hot, so feel free to use less, if you prefer. Small, fat chillies are usually milder than long, thin ones.

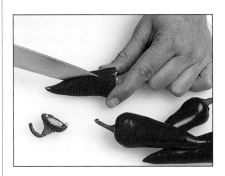

1 Remove the stalks, then slice the chillies lengthways.

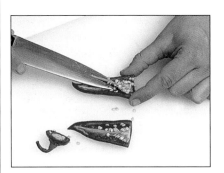

2 Scrape out the pith and seeds from the chillies, then slice, shred or chop the flesh as required. The seeds can be either discarded or added to the dish, depending on the amount of heat that is required.

PREPARING DRIED CHILLIES

Dried chillies are available from Asian food stores and larger supermarkets.

1 Remove the stems and seeds and snap each chilli into two or three pieces. Put these in a bowl, pour over hot water to cover and leave to stand for 30 minutes.

2 Drain, reserving the soaking water if it can usefully be added to the dish. Use the pieces of chilli as they are, or chop them finely.

MAKING CHILLI FLOWERS

Thai cooks are famous for their beautiful presentation, and often garnish platters with chilli flowers, which are quite simple to make.

1 Holding each chilli in turn by the stem, slit it in half lengthways.

2 Keeping the stem end of the chilli intact, cut it lengthways into strips.

3 Put the chillies in a bowl of iced water, cover and chill for 3–4 hours. The cut chilli strips will curl back to resemble flower petals. Drain well on kitchen paper and use as a garnish. Small chillies may be very hot, so don't be tempted to eat the flowers.

Right: Fresh green chillies

Chillies

Hot chillies and sweet (bell) peppers belong to the same genus, capsicum, and there are scores of varieties. Like sweet peppers, many chillies start out green and ripen to red, while others change from yellow to red and finally to brown or even black, so what might appear to be a basket of assorted chillies could turn out to be the same type of chilli in varying degrees of ripeness. Size also varies. Although South-east Asian cooks tend to use them fresh, chillies are also available dried.

Always treat chillies with caution, as some varieties can be extremely fiery. Much of the severe heat is contained in the seeds, so remove these before use if you prefer a milder flavour. Chillies and other spicy foods are in fact perfect for hot climates because they encourage blood to rush to the surface of the skin, and therefore promote cooling. Chillies

Below: Medium red chillies

CHILLI PASTE

Ready-made chilli paste is sold in jars. However, it is easy to make at home. Simply halve and seed fresh chillies, then place them in a food processor and purée to a smooth paste. A chopped onion can be added to the processor to add bulk to the paste. Store small amounts of the paste in the refrigerator for up to 1 week, or spoon into containers, and freeze for up to 6 months. *Sambal oelek*, an Indonesian chilli sauce, is made in a similar way, but first the chillies are blanched.

are used fresh in South-east Asia in sauces and salads, and are an essential ingredient in Indonesian sambals. They also find their way into a variety of cooked dishes, including stocks, soups, braised dishes, curries and stir-fries, with or without the seeds. Where just a hint of heat is required, chillies are added whole to a dish, then removed just before serving.

Lemon grass

Widely used throughout South-east Asia, lemon grass is an important ingredient in soups, sauces, stir-fries, curries, salads, pickles and marinades. It is a perfect partner for coconut milk, especially in fish, shellfish and chicken dishes. It has a clean, intense lemon flavour with a hint of ginger but none of the acidity associated with lemon or grapefruit. Thai cooks often start a stir-fry by adding a few sliced rings of lemon grass and perhaps a little grated or chopped fresh root ginger or galangal to the oil.

Ground dried lemon grass, also known as serai powder, can be used instead of fresh. As a guide, about 5ml/ 1 tsp powder is equivalent to 1 fresh stalk. Whole and dried chopped stalks

are also available in jars from Asian food stores and larger supermarkets, as are jars of lemon grass paste.

There are two main ways of using lemon grass. The stalk can be bruised, then cooked slowly in a soup or stew until it releases all its flavour and is removed, or the tender portions of the lemon grass can be sliced or finely chopped, then stir-fried or used in a salad or braised dish. Often one stalk will serve both purposes; the tougher top end is used for the background flavouring while the tender lower portion forms the focal point of a dish.

Kaffir limes

These fruits are not true limes, but belong to a subspecies of the citrus family. Native to South-east Asia, kaffir lime leaves are synonymous with Thai cooking, and are also used in Indonesia, Malaysia, Burma and Vietnam. Only the rind and leaves are used, the fruit and juice are not eaten. The scented bouquet is citrus, and the full lemon flavour is released when the leaves are torn or shredded. The leaves are used in soups and curries. The finely grated rind is sometimes added to fish or chicken dishes.

Curry leaves

These are the shiny green leaves of a hardwood tree that is indigenous to India. Although they look like bay leaves, their flavour is very different. They are used in Indian cooking, especially in south India and Sri Lanka, and were first introduced to Malaysia by Tamil migrants. The spear-shaped

Left: Fresh lemon grass stalks

Above: Kaffir limes and leaves

leaves grow on a thin stem. They have an intriguing warm fragrance, with just a hint of sweet, green pepper or tangerine. The full flavour is released when the leaves are bruised. When added to curries or braised dishes, they impart a distinctive flavour. Dried curry leaves come a very poor second to fresh, and they rapidly lose their fragrance.

MAKING A LEMON GRASS BRUSH

To make a lemon stalk into a basting brush, trim off the bottom 5cm/2in of the stalk to use in a recipe, then flatten the cut end of the remaining stalk using a cleaver or pestle to produce a fibrous brush. Use the brush to baste grilled (broiled) foods.

Mint

The Asian variety of mint is much more strongly flavoured than most European types, and is slightly sweet tasting, imparting a cool aftertaste and a stimulating aroma. Mint is an essential ingredient in Vietnamese cooking, and it was they who introduced it to the Thais. As it has such a dominant flavour, mint is seldom used with other herbs.

Coriander

This beautifully aromatic herb is widely used in South-east Asian cooking for its wonderful flavour. Fresh coriander (cilantro) also makes an attractive garnish, and it freezes well. Available all over South-east Asia, coriander seeds are more often used than fresh coriander leaves in Indonesia.

Basil

This is one of the oldest herbs known to man, and is thought to have originated in India. However, basil is not used in India as much as it is in the rest of South-east Asia. It is important in Laos, Vietnam and Cambodia, but it is in Thailand that basil is most widely used, and for this reason it is the varieties of basil favoured by the Thais that are most often seen in Asian food stores. If you cannot find Thai basil, any European variety can be used, but the flavour will not be the same, and you should use a little more than the amount

Below: Fresh coriander

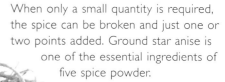

recommended. Basil is best used fresh, but freeze-dried leaves are also available from supermarkets. It is added to curries and salads, as an ingredient and as a garnish. Avoid chopping basil leaves, but tear them into pieces or add them to the dish whole.

Star anise

This unusual star-shaped spice comes from an evergreen tree native to South-east China and Vietnam. The points of the star contain amber seeds. Both the seeds and the husk are used for the ground spice. Star anise both smells and tastes like liquorice, and its aromatic flavour complements all rich meats. It is used to flavour beef soups in Vietnam, and is used in light desserts, such as fruit salads.

Star anise can be added whole, and it looks so attractive that it is often left in a dish when serving.

When only a small quantity is required, the spice can be broken and just one or two points added. Ground star anise is one of the essential ingredients of five spice powder.

Cloves

These are unopened flower buds of a tree that is a member of the myrtle family. Cloves originated in the Spice Islands in Indonesia and were taken to the Seychelles and Mauritius in the 18th century. Cloves have an intense fragrance and an aromatic flavour that can be fiery. They also have astringent properties. In South-east Asia, cloves are mainly used in savoury dishes, and their warm, aromatic flavour complements rich meats. Thai cooks use cloves to cut the rich flavour of duck, and also use them with tomatoes, salty vegetables and in ham or pork dishes. Ground cloves are an essential ingredient in many curry spice mixtures.

Above: Cloves

Below: Fresh Thai basil

Above: Star anise

Cinnamon

The sweet and fragrant bouquet of cinnamon comes from an essential oil, oil of cinnamon, which is used medicinally. The flavour is warm and aromatic, and has universal appeal as a flavouring in sweet and savoury dishes, and cakes and breads. In South-east Asia, the sticks are used in spicy meat dishes, often with star anise, with which cinnamon has an affinity. Add the whole or broken cinnamon stick as directed in the recipe. Pure ground cinnamon is rarely used in Asian cooking.

Cassia

Sometimes known as Chinese cinnamon, cassia smells rather like cinnamon, but is more pungent. Cracked cassia quills and cassia buds (which look like cloves) are used in the East to give a warm aromatic flavour to pickles, curries and meat dishes. Cassia is quite tough. Break the pieces as required with the end of a rolling pin or put them in a mortar and use a pestle to shatter them. Where ground cassia is required, it is best to buy it in that form.

Cumin

This is believed to have originated in the eastern Mediterranean, but is now widely cultivated . The plant is a member of the parsley family, but only the seeds (whole or ground) are used in cooking.

Above: Ground cinnamon and cinnamon sticks

Cumin has a sweet, warm and spicy aroma. The flavour is pungent but not harsh. It is often partnered with whole or ground coriander seeds. Indian cooks are particularly partial to cumin, and it was they who introduced the spice to Singapore, Malaysia and Indonesia.

To bring out the full flavour, the seeds are often dry-fried. They are then used whole, or ground in a spice mill or using a mortar and pestle.

Above: Ground cumin and cumin seeds

Cardamom

Cardamom belongs to the ginger family. It is largely grown for its pods, although Thai cooks sometimes use the leaves for flavouring. The pods are either added whole to spicy dishes, or opened so that the tiny dark seeds can be extracted. The most familiar pods are pale green, and there are also white pods, which are bleached green ones. Black cardamoms, which come from Vietnam and India, are large and coarse. They taste quite different, and are used in red meat dishes. Cardamoms are sweet, pungent and aromatic. They have a warm flavour, with hints of lemon and eucalyptus.

Left: Ground cassia and cassia quills

Above: From left, green and brown cardamom pods

Left: Clockwise from top, brown, black and white mustard seeds

Mustard seeds

These seeds have no aroma in their raw state but when they are roasted they develop a rich, nutty smell. The famous hot taste comes from an enzyme in the seeds, which is only activated when they are crushed and mixed with warm water. Brown mustard seeds, which have largely replaced the black seeds, are not as intensely pungent. White mustard seeds are larger than the other varieties and a little milder.

Throughout Asia, mustard seeds are used for pickling and seasoning, while whole mustard seeds are often used in vegetable and dhal dishes.

Fennel seeds

Sweet, warm and aromatic, fennel seeds have a distinct anise flavour. Fennel seeds are a constituent in many spice mixtures, especially those that are intended to be used with fish or shellfish.

Fennel seeds should be dry-fried before grinding so that the full flavour of the spice is released.

Annatto seeds

The shrub from which the annatto seeds are taken has heart-shaped, glossy leaves and spectacular, pink, rose-like flowers. The plant produces a heart-shaped fruit capsule, which splits itself in half when ripe to reveal fifty or more seeds. The Spanish introduced the seeds to the Philippines, and annatto seeds are widely used in Filipino dishes.

Annatto seeds are brick-red and triangular in shape, with a peppery flavour and bouquet, and just a hint of nutmeg in their aroma. The seeds can be infused in hot water, and will impart a rich red colour to oil when fried for a few minutes. Add the water or oil to rice dishes and use in place of saffron.

Peppercorns

Black peppercorns have an earthy aroma, which is particularly noticeable when they are crushed. The flavour is hot and pungent. White peppercorns are slightly milder.

Pepper can be used before, during and after cooking. Its value is legendary, for it not only has its own flavour, but has the ability to enhance the flavour of other ingredients in a dish.

Below: From left, white and black peppercorns

DRY FRYING MUSTARD SEEDS

Mustard seeds have almost no smell until they are heated so, before adding them to dishes, they should be dry-fried to heighten their aroma.

1 Heat a little sunflower oil in a wok or large pan. Add the seeds and shake the pan over the heat, stirring occasionally, until they start to change colour.

2 Have a pan lid to hand so that you are ready to prevent the mustard seeds from popping out of the pan.

GRINDING SPICES

Spices are often crushed or ground to release their flavour. Only a few, notably mace, dried ginger and turmeric, cinnamon and cassia, are difficult to grind at home and should be bought in powdered form. For the best flavour, grind spices as you need them. Don't grind them more than a day or two in advance.

DRY-FRYING WHOLE SPICES

Many whole spices benefit from being dry-fried before they are ground. This makes sure that no surface moisture remains, and it heightens and develops the flavour. To dry-fry spices, heat a wok or heavy pan for 1 minute, then add the spices. Cook for 2–3 minutes, stirring and shaking the pan constantly to prevent the spices from scorching. When the spices start to give off a warm, rich aroma, remove the pan from the heat and tip the spices into a spice mill or a mortar, and process or grind with a pestle. Purists recommend that each spice is dry-fried separately, but several spices can be cooked together, if watched over closely.
All spices react differently to heat, so follow these basic guidelines for best results:
• Coriander seeds often provide the dominant flavour, especially in powders from Southern India and Singapore. Shake the pan well to keep the seeds on the move, and remove them from the heat when they start to give off a mild, sweet, orangey perfume.
• Dried chillies can be roasted in a cool oven, but it is better to sear them in a heavy pan, where you can keep an eye on them. Place the pan over a medium heat for 2–3 minutes, until the chillies soften and puff up. Do not let them burn, or the flavour will be ruined. Transfer to a plate immediately to stop them overheating or burning.
• Cumin seeds should be dry-fried in a pan, and will be ready for grinding when the seeds release their aroma, usually within 40–50 seconds.
• Black peppercorns need gentle dry-frying, just to heighten the flavour.
• Fenugreek needs to be watched carefully as it will become bitter if it is dry-fried for too long. It is ready when it turns brownish yellow.
• Curry leaves can be dry-fried over a cool to medium heat when fresh. Grind or pound them, using a mortar and pestle, to release their characteristic flavour, then mix them with the other spices. This works well if you are making a curry powder or paste that is to be used immediately, but if it is to be kept for more than 24 hours, make up the powder, then add the whole fresh or frozen leaves just before you are ready to use it. Remove the leaves before serving the curry. Avoid using dried curry leaves if possible, as they will have lost most of their flavour in the dehydration process.

Right: From top, compressed tamarind, compressed tamarind block and dried tamarind slices

Tamarind

Although tamarind doesn't have much of an aroma, its flavour is tart, sour, fruity and refreshing. It is used in many South-east Asian curries, chutneys and dhals, and is an essential ingredient of Thai hot and sour soups. Blocks of compressed tamarind and slices of dried tamarind have been available for a while, but it is now also possible to buy jars of fresh tamarind and cartons of tamarind concentrate and paste, which require less preparation time. There really is no substitute for tamarind. Some recipes may suggest using vinegar or lemon or lime juice instead, but the results will not compare with using the real thing.
Compressed tamarind is sold in a solid block and looks rather like dried dates.

To prepare it, tear off a piece that is roughly equivalent to 15ml/1 tbsp and soak it in 150ml/¼ pint/⅔ cup warm water for 10 minutes. Swirl the tamarind around with your fingers so that the pulp is released from the seeds. Using a nylon sieve, strain the juice into a jug (pitcher). Discard the contents of the sieve and use the liquid as required.
Tamarind slices look a little like dried apple slices. Place them in a small bowl, then pour over enough warm water to cover and leave to soak for 30 minutes to extract the flavour, squeeze the tamarind slices with your fingers, then strain the juice into a jug.
Tamarind concentrate or paste is sold in Asian food stores, and is a quick and convenient alternative to compressed

tamarind and tamarind slices. To prepare, mix 15ml/1 tbsp concentrate or paste with 60–90ml/4–6 tbsp warm water. Stir briskly until dissolved, then use as required in the recipe. Any leftover liquid can be stored in the refrigerator and used for another recipe.

CURRY POWDERS and PASTES

Curry powders and pastes are spice blends that are used as the basis of a curry. Traditionally, these mixtures would be prepared as needed, using fresh ingredients, but for convenience a wide variety of prepared pastes and powders are now available commercially, and most supermarket shelves carry a wealth of different spice mixtures from all parts of the globe. However, for enthusiastic cooks it is fun and a creative challenge to make up your own curry powders and pastes. Keep experimenting until you find the balance of spicing that suits you and your family. It is perfectly possible to mix ground spices, but it is more satisfying (and much more satisfactory in terms of flavour) to start with whole spices.

Curry powders

The word curry evolved from the Tamil word *kaari*, meaning any food cooked in a sauce. There is little doubt that curry powder, a ready-made blend of spices, was an early convenience food, prepared for merchants, sailors and military men who had served in the East and wished to bring these exotic flavours home.

Simple curry powder

This Malayan Chinese spice mixture is good for poultry, especially chicken, and robust fish curries.

MAKES ABOUT 60ML/4 TBSP

2 dried red chillies
6 whole cloves
1 small cinnamon stick
5ml/1 tsp coriander seeds
5ml/1 tsp fennel seeds
10ml/2 tsp Sichuan peppercorns
2.5ml/½ tsp freshly grated nutmeg
5ml/1 tsp ground star anise
5ml/1 tsp ground turmeric

WATCHPOINTS

• Ensure that you wash your hands, and the chopping board and other utensils thoroughly after preparing chillies.
• If your skin is particularly sensitive, then you should wear rubber gloves while you are preparing the chillies.

1 Remove the seeds from the dried chillies using the point of a knife, and discard any stems. If you prefer a very hot and punchy spice mixture, then retain some or all of the chilli seeds.

2 Put the chillies, cloves, cinnamon, coriander, fennel seeds and Sichuan peppercorns in a wok or large pan. Dry-fry the spices, tossing them around the pan frequently until they start to release a rich, spicy aroma.

3 Grind the spices to a smooth powder in a mortar, using a pestle. Alternatively, use a spice mill, or an electric coffee grinder that is reserved for the purpose.

4 Add the grated nutmeg, star anise and turmeric. Use immediately or store in an airtight jar away from strong light.

SEVEN-SEAS CURRY POWDER

Seven-seas Curry Powder is a mild spice blend used in Indonesian and Malaysian curries. The name refers to the seven seas, including the Andaman and South China Sea, that converge on the shores of Malaysia and the islands of Indonesia.

To make the powder, bruise 6–8 cardamom pods and put them in a wok with 90ml/6 tbsp coriander seeds, 45ml/3 tbsp cumin seeds, 22.5ml/1½ tbsp celery seeds, 5cm/2in piece cinnamon stick, 6–8 cloves and 15ml/1 tbsp chilli powder. Dry-fry until the rich aroma is released.

Curry pastes

On market stalls throughout South-east Asia are mounds of pounded wet spices: lemon grass, chilli, ginger, garlic, galangal, shallots and tamarind. After purchasing meat, chicken or fish, all the cook has to do is to call on the spice seller. He or she will ask a few questions: "What sort of curry is it to be? Hot or mild? How many servings?" Having ascertained the answers and perhaps exchanged a few more pleasantries, the appropriate quantities of each spice will be scooped on to a banana leaf and folded into a neat cone, ready to be taken home.

We may not be able to buy our ingredients in such colourful surroundings, but Western supermarkets now stock some very good ready-made pastes, or you can make your own at home. By experimenting, you will find the balance of flavours you like, and can then make your favourite mixtures in bulk. Store surplus curry paste in in the freezer.

COOK'S TIP

If you grind wet spices a lot, you may find it useful to invest in a traditional Asian mortar, made from granite, with a rough, pitted or ridged bowl, which helps to hold the ingredients while they are being pounded with the pestle. Alternatively, for speed, you can use a food processor or blender instead of a mortar and pestle.

Red curry paste

This Thai paste was named after the colour of the chillies used to prepare it. For a hotter paste, add a few chilli seeds.

MAKES ABOUT 175G/6OZ/¾ CUP

5ml/1 tsp coriander seeds, roasted
2.5ml/½ tsp cumin seeds, roasted
12–15 fresh red chillies, seeded and
roughly chopped
4 shallots, thinly sliced
2 garlic cloves, chopped
15ml/1 tbsp peeled and
  chopped fresh galangal
2 lemon grass stalks, chopped
4 fresh coriander roots
10 black peppercorns
good pinch of ground cinnamon
5ml/1 tsp ground turmeric
2.5ml/½ tsp shrimp paste
5ml/1 tsp salt
30ml/2 tbsp vegetable oil

1 Put all the ingredients except the oil in a mortar or food processor and pound or process to a paste.

2 Add the oil, a little at a time, mixing or processing well after each addition. Transfer to a glass jar, and keep in the refrigerator until ready to use.

VARIATIONS

• For Green Curry Paste, process 12–15 green chillies, 2 chopped lemon grass stalks, 3 sliced shallots, 2 garlic cloves, 15ml/1 tbsp chopped galangal, 4 chopped kaffir lime leaves, 2.5ml/½ tsp grated kaffir rind, 5ml/1 tsp each of chopped coriander root, salt, roasted coriander seeds, roasted cumin seeds and shrimp paste, 15ml/1 tbsp granulated sugar, 6 black peppercorns and 15ml/ 1 tbsp vegetable oil until a paste forms.
• For Yellow Curry Paste, process 6–8 yellow chillies, 1 chopped lemon grass stalk, 4 sliced shallots, 4 garlic cloves, 15ml/1 tbsp chopped fresh root ginger, 5ml/1 tsp coriander seeds, 5ml/ 1 tsp each of mustard powder and salt, 2.5ml/½ tsp ground cinnamon, 15ml/ 1 tbsp light brown sugar and 30ml/2 tbsp vegetable oil until a paste forms.

Mussaman curry paste

This hot and spicy paste is used to make the Thai version of a Muslim curry, which is traditionally made with beef, but can also be made with other meats such as chicken or lamb.

MAKES ABOUT 175G/6OZ/¾ CUP

12 large dried red chillies
1 lemon grass stalk
60ml/4 tbsp chopped shallots
5 garlic cloves, roughly chopped
10ml/2 tsp chopped fresh galangal
5ml/1 tsp cumin seeds
15ml/1 tbsp coriander seeds
2 cloves
6 black peppercorns
5ml/1 tsp shrimp paste,
  prepared
5ml/1 tsp salt
5ml/1 tsp granulated sugar
30ml/2 tbsp vegetable oil

1 Carefully remove the seeds from the dried chillies and discard. Soak the chillies in a bowl of hot water for about 15 minutes.

2 Trim the root end from the lemon grass stalk and slice the lower 5cm/2in of the stalk into small pieces.

3 Place the chopped lemon grass in a dry wok over a low heat, and then add the chopped shallots, garlic and galangal and dry-fry for 2–3 minutes.

4 Stir in the cumin seeds, coriander seeds, cloves and peppercorns and continue to dry-fry over a low heat for 5–6 minutes, stirring constantly. Spoon the mixture into a large mortar.

5 Drain the chillies and add them to the mortar. Grind finely, using the pestle, then add the prepared shrimp paste, salt, sugar and oil and pound again until the mixture forms a rough paste. Use as required, then spoon any leftover paste into a jar, seal tightly and store in the refrigerator for up to 4 months.

COOK'S TIPS

• Preparing a double or larger quantity of paste in a food processor or blender makes the blending of the ingredients easier and the paste will be smoother.
• For the best results, before you start to process the ingredients, slice them up in the following order: galangal, lemon grass, fresh ginger and turmeric, chillies, nuts, shrimp paste, garlic and shallots. Add some of the oil (or coconut cream, if that is to be your frying medium) to the food processor if the mixture is a bit sluggish. If you do this, remember to use less oil or coconut cream when you fry the curry paste to eliminate the raw taste of the ingredients before adding the meat, poultry, fish or vegetables.

PREPARING SHRIMP PASTE

Shrimp paste is a seasoning made from fermented shrimps. It can be bought in Asian food stores. Unless it is to be fried as part of a recipe, it should always be lightly cooked before use.

If you have a gas cooker, simply mould the shrimp paste on to a metal skewer and rotate over a low gas flame, or heat under the grill of an electric cooker, until the outside begins to look crusty but not burnt.

ADDITIONAL INGREDIENTS

Many of the basic ingredients called for in South-east Asian curry recipes will store very well. Others should be bought fresh, as needed.

Peanuts

Also known as groundnuts or monkey nuts, peanuts are eaten as a snack food, and as ingredients in salads and curries . In Indonesia and Malaysia, roasted peanuts, pounded to a paste, are the basis for satay sauce.

Above: Whole peanuts

Palm sugar

This strongly flavoured brown sugar is made from the sap of the coconut palm tree. It is sold in Asian food stores. Dark brown sugar can be used as a substitute.

Soy sauce

This is made from fermented soya beans, wheat grain, salt and water. There are two main varieties: thick, sometimes referred to as black or dark, and thin, curiously referred to as white or light. In Indonesia, a soy sauce called kecap manis is preferred, because it is thicker and sweeter.

Brown bean sauce

Made from salted, fermented soy beans, this is a popular flavouring in Asian cooking. Yellow bean sauce is also available.

Rice wine vinegar

Japanese rice wine vinegar is used in South-east Asia for dipping sauces and preserving. Cider vinegar and any mild, plain white vinegar can be used instead.

Shrimp paste

An essential ingredient common to the countries of South-east Asia, this paste is also known as *terasi*, *blachan* and *balachan*. It is made from fermented shrimps or prawns, with salt, pounded into a paste and sold in blocks. Wrap a cube in a foil parcel and place in a dry pan over a low heat for 5 minutes, turning from time to time. This takes away the rawness from the paste and avoids filling the kitchen with the strong smell. If the paste is to be fried, this initial cooking is not needed.

Fish sauce

The most commonly used flavouring in Thai cooking is fish sauce, which is known in Thailand as *nam pla*. It is made from salted anchovies, and may be sold as anchovy sauce in Asian stores. Fish sauce has a strong salty flavour, and is used in the same way as soy sauce.

Salted eggs

This is the traditional way to preserve duck eggs in South-east Asia. The eggs are sold in Asian stores, often covered in a layer of charcoal ash. Rub off the ash under running water, then hard-boil (hard-cook) the eggs.

Below: Dark and light soy sauce

Beancurd/tofu and tempeh

These fragile looking 7.5cm/3in cubes are available fresh. Beancurd, which is also known by its Japanese name, tofu, is made in a similar way to soft cheese, but uses soya bean milk instead of dairy milk, set with gypsum, and for this reason it is popular with vegetarians and vegans, who do not eat dairy foods. In spite of its bland flavour, beancurd is bursting with protein, and will absorb flavours of other ingredients quickly.

Tempeh is an Indonesian speciality. It is made from fermented soya beans, to give a cake that is packed full of protein, iron and vitamin B. Add it to dishes as directed on the packet.

Below: Clockwise from left, silken tofu, beancurd skins, firm tofu and deep-fried tofu.

FRUITS and VEGETABLES

There are several key fruit and vegetable ingredients used in South-east Asian cooking, and most of these are now available from Western supermarkets.

Banana leaves
The large green leaves of the banana tree are South-east Asia's answer to kitchen foil. Make the leaves more pliable by plunging them into boiling water. Place the ingredients for cooking inside, make into a parcel and secure with a skewer. Food wrapped in this way is flavoured by the leaf itself.

Pandan leaves
These leaves impart a warm aroma when cooked. Available fresh, in bunches, pandan (screwpine) leaves are used to flavour rice and desserts. Pull the tines of a fork through a leaf to tear it and release the flavour, and tie the leaf in a knot so that it is easy to remove. Screwpine essence (extract) can be used as an alternative.

Bangkuang (yambean)
These are the same shape as a turnip but with a smooth, light golden skin, which should be peeled thinly. The texture is somewhere between that of an apple and a hard pear. Peel the bangkuang and cut in julienne strips, to use in stir-fries, spring rolls or salads.

Beansprouts
Readily available, beansprouts are widely used in Asian cooking, where they add a crunchy texture and delicate flavour to soups, salads and stir-fries. Most beansprouts come from mung beans, although soya beans are also sold. Both can be sprouted at home. Store beansprouts in the refrigerator in a covered container for 2–3 days.

Bamboo shoots
The edible young shoots of the bamboo plant are sold fresh or canned; fresh shoots take a long time to cook, but taste much better than the canned variety; if buying canned shoots, look for the whole ones, which are better quality than the ready-sliced variety.

Above: Beansprouts

Chayote
This pear-shaped vegetable can be eaten raw or cooked, and is often stir-fried or simmered in soups. Chayote has a mild taste not unlike courgette (zucchini). It is usually cooked with strong seasonings such as garlic, ginger and chillies.

Chinese leaves
This versatile vegetable, known as Chinese cabbage in the United States, can be used in stir-fries, stews, curries or soups. It will absorb the flavours of other ingredients, while retaining its own mild, cabbage flavour and crunchy texture.

Sweet potatoes
Several varieties of sweet potatoes are grown all over South-east Asia. After peeling, they are sliced and stir-fried, or braised with seasoning amd spices.

Aubergines
Many varieties of aubergine (eggplant) are grown in South-east Asia, from tiny pea aubergines, which are added at the end of cooking, to white, yellow or green aubergines. When these types are unavailable, use the purple variety.

Onions
The versatile onion is an important flavouring agent in Asian cooking, and an essential ingredient in sauces, curries and stews. Only spring onions (scallions) are usually eaten as a vegetable, although deep-fried onions are a popular garnish. Shallots are used extensively in Thai dishes in place of onions.

Papaya
In South-east Asia, papaya is eaten both as a fruit and a vegetable. Unripe green papayas are served raw in salads or used in pickles, while papayas that are not too ripe are added to soups, curries and seafood dishes. The ripe fruit is eaten as a dessert. Both the juice and skin of papaya are also used to tenderize meat.

Coconut
This versatile fruit is one of the hallmarks of South-east Asian cooking. Coconut milk is used as a cooking medium, in place of stock, and is added at the end of cooking to enrich curries; canned milk is sold commercially, but it can also be made at home, using desiccated (dry, unsweetened, shredded) coconut. If the milk is left to stand, coconut cream will rise to the surface. Creamed coconut is sold in blocks or in powdered form. Small quantities are used to enrich and thicken dishes at the end of cooking.

MAKING COCONUT MILK
Coconut milk can be made at home from desiccated coconut. Make as much or as little as you like, varying the quantities accordingly.

Tip 225g/8oz/2⅔ cups desiccated coconut into the bowl of a food processor and pour over 450ml/¾ pint/scant 2 cups boiling water. Process for 20–30 seconds and allow to cool.

Place a sieve lined with muslin (cheesecloth) over a large bowl in the sink. Ladle some of the softened coconut into the muslin.

Bring up the ends of the cloth and twist it over the sieve to extract as much of the liquid as possible. Discard the spent coconut. Store the coconut milk in the refrigerator. Use as directed in the recipes.

RICE and NOODLES

The unassertive flavour of rice and noodles makes them perfect partners for spicy curry dishes. Rice is the staple grain of the whole of Asia, but noodles also form an important part of the daily diet throughout the region.

Rice

A bowl of rice is eaten at every meal throughout South-east Asia, including breakfast. It is usually served simply boiled or steamed, although in some countries coconut milk is used instead of water for

Right: Thai fragrant rice

some dishes. There are thousands of varieties of rice in the major rice-growing regions of South-east Asia, although people generally only eat the rice that is grown locally. Types of rice are classified by region, by colour, by cooking properties or even by price, but the most common classification is by the length of grain, which can be long, medium or short. As a general rule, long and medium grain rices are used in South-east Asia for savoury dishes, while short grain rice is used for puddings and desserts.

Long grain rices

There are many strains of long grain rice, and it is the most common rice in South-east Asia, partly because it can be used in a variety of recipes. White long grain rice has had its husk, bran and germ removed. It is light and fluffy when cooked, with a bland flavour. Brown long grain rice has had only its outer husk removed, which gives it a chewy texture and nutty flavour. It takes longer to cook than white long grain rice, but contains more fibre, vitamins and minerals.

Thai fragrant rice is a long grain rice cultivated in Thailand, and it is widely used throughout South-east Asia. The rice has a distinctive scent of jasmine (it is also known as jasmine rice) and a perfumed flavour, for which it is highly prized. Once cooked, the grains become slightly sticky.

Glutinous rice

This short grain rice is also known as sticky or waxy rice because of the way the grains stick together after cooking. White glutinous rice is the most common type in South-east Asia, but there is also a black glutinous rice, which retains the husk and has a nutty flavour. A pinkish-red variety is cultivated on the banks of the River Yangtze in China.

COOKING BOILED RICE

Always use a tight-fitting lid for your rice pan. If you do not have a lid that fits tightly, wrap a dishtowel around the lid or put some foil between the lid and the pan. Try not to remove the lid until the rice is cooked. (The advantage of using a lid is that you can tell when the rice is ready because steam begins to escape, visibly and rapidly, from underneath.) As a guide, allow 75g/3oz/scant ½ cup rice per person.

Put the dry rice in a colander and rinse it under cold running water until the water runs clear. Then place the rice in a large pan and pour in enough cold water to come 2cm/¾in above the surface of the rice. Add a pinch of salt and, if you like, 5ml/1 tsp vegetable oil, stir once and bring to the boil. Stir once more, reduce the heat to low and cover the pan with the lid. Cook the rice for 12–15 minutes, then turn off the heat and leave the rice to stand, still covered, for 10 minutes. Before serving, fluff up the rice with a fork or a slotted rice spoon.

COOKING FRIED RICE

Fried rice is usually served as a snack on its own, or as part of a special buffet dinner. For best results, use cold, firm, cooked rice.

1 Stir-fry any uncooked meat in oil in a wok, then add chopped onions. Transfer to a plate and set aside.

2 Add beaten egg to the frying pan and scramble with sliced spring onions (scallions). Add spices and flavourings such as soy sauce, rice wine, chopped herbs, fresh chillies, or tomato purée (paste).

3 Tip the cold rice into the wok and mix with the egg. Return any cooked meats or seafood to the wok. Cook until heated through.

Noodles

These are second only to rice as a staple food in South-east Asia. Unlike rice, however, which is served plain to be eaten with cooked dishes, noodles are usually cooked with other ingredients. For this reason, they are seldon served as accompaniments, but are eaten on their own as light meals or snacks. Noodle street vendors are a common sight, particularly in Thailand.

South-east Asian noodles are made from flour pastes, including wheat, rice and mung bean. Some are plain; others are enriched with egg. All are easy to prepare, but see individual recipes for advice as some types benefit from being soaked before cooking. Both fresh and dried noodles have to be cooked in boiling water; they are then served in one of three ways: in a soup, braised in a broth and eaten with a sauce, or fried.

Wheat noodles

Plain noodles are made from strong plain wheat flour, and are available flat or round, in a variety of thicknesses.

Above: *Cellophane noodles*

Egg noodles are far more common than plain wheat noodles, and are sold in various thicknesses, fresh or dried.

Rice noodles

These noodles, sometimes called rice sticks, are derived from a paste made from whole rice grains, and are sold in various widths, fresh and dried. Rice noodles are partly cooked when they are made, and they need only to be soaked to soften them before use.

Below: *Fresh egg noodles come in various thicknesses.*

PREPARING NOODLES

• Add dried egg noodles to a pan of salted boiling water and cook for 3–5 minutes. Stir to prevent the noodles from settling on the base of the pan. Drain and rinse with cold water, to wash out starch. Fresh egg noodles take 1 minute to cook in salted, fast-boiling water. Drain.

• Rice noodles can be soaked ahead of cooking, either in cold water for some time or in warm water for just a few minutes. Plunge into fast-boiling, salted water. Return to the boil, then remove from the heat and leave for 2 minutes, until cooked. Test one piece and then drain and rinse well with cold water.

• Soak cellophane noodles in cold water, cut into lengths and place in boiling water for 1 minute. Drain well and use as required.

Cellophane noodles

These are made with green mung bean flour, the same beans as those used for sprouting. Although thin, the strands are firm and will not become soggy when cooked. Cellophane noodles are almost tasteless, although they are never served solo but are always used as an ingredient in a dish, usually in vegetarian cooking.

Above: *Thick and thin Thai noodles.*

EQUIPMENT and UTENSILS

The equipment in the average Western kitchen will be perfectly adequate for most of the recipes in this book, particularly now that the wok has become an indispensable item in many households. There are some items, however, that will make cooking South-east Asian food easier and more pleasurable. The fact that many of these simple pieces of equipment also look good, and instantly establish you as an adventurous cook in the eyes of your friends, is a bonus.

The best way to build up your store of specialist items is to start slowly, with a few basics such as a cleaver, bamboo grater and wok, then gradually add extra pieces as you experiment with different styles of cooking. The design of many utensils has not changed in centuries, and items made from basic materials are often more effective than modern equivalents.

Cleaver

To Western cooks, a cleaver can seem rather intimidating. In reality, cleavers are among the most useful pieces of equipment ever invented. They come in several sizes and weights. Number one is the heaviest, with a blade 23cm/9in long and 10cm/4in wide, and weighing up to 1kg/2¼lb. At the other end of the scale, number three has a shorter, narrower blade and is only half as heavy. Number two is the cook's favourite because of its many uses. The back of the blade is used for pounding and tenderizing, and the flat for crushing and transporting. Even the handle has more than one purpose – its end can be used as a pestle.

Cleavers can be made of carbonized steel with wooden handles, or of stainless steel with metal or wooden handles. Choose the one you are comfortable with. Hold it in your hand and feel the weight; it should be neither too heavy nor too light. One point to remember is that a stainless steel cleaver will require frequent sharpening if it is to stay razor sharp. To prevent a carbonized

Below: Cleaver

Below: Traditional bamboo grater

steel blade from rusting, wipe it dry after every use, then give it a thin coating of vegetable oil. Cleavers should always be sharpened on whetstone, never with a steel sharpener. The cleaver is not as dangerous as it looks, if handled with care. Learn to regard it as just another kitchen knife, and you will be rewarded with very satisfactory results.

Chopping block

The traditional chopping block in South-east Asia is simply a cross-section of a tree trunk, usually hardwood. A large rectangular cutting board of hardwood can be used instead, but make sure it is at least 5cm/2in thick or it may not be able to take a blow from a cleaver. Acrylic boards are also available.

Season a chopping block with vegetable oil on both sides to prevent it from splitting. Let it absorb as much oil as it will take, then clean the block with salt and water and dry it thoroughly. After each use, scrape the surface with the back of your cleaver, then wipe it down with a cloth. Never immerse a wooden block in water.

Grater

Traditional graters, used for preparing ginger, galangal and daikon (mooli), are made from wood or bamboo, but a metal cheese grater makes a satisfactory substitute.

Mortar and pestle

South-east Asian cooks prefer granite or stone mortars and pestles, since these have rough surfaces which help to grip the ingredients. Bigger, flat-bowled mortars are good for making spice pastes that contain large amounts of fresh spices, onion, herbs and garlic.

Spice mill

If you are going to grind a lot of spices, a spice mill will prove useful. An electric coffee grinder works well for this purpose, but it is a good idea to reserve the mill for spices only.

Wok

In the Philippines, the traditional cooking pot is made of clay. Modern households, however, prefer to use a wok, known as a *carajay* (pronounced carahai). The wok is also widely used in Indonesia, where it is known as a *wajan*, and in Malaysia, where it is called a *kulai*.

It is not surprising that the wok has become a universal favourite, for it is remarkably versatile. The rounded bottom was originally designed to

Below: Traditional granite mortar and pestle

Left: Carbonized steel woks

Below: Wok lid and utensils

vegetable oil. After each use, wash the wok with hot water, but never use detergent as this would remove the seasoning and cause the wok to rust. Any food that sticks to the wok should be scraped off with a non-metal scourer, and the wok should then be rinsed and dried over a low heat. Before being put away, a little oil should always be rubbed into the surface of the wok.

Wok tools

Some wok sets come with a spatula and ladle made from cast iron or stainless steel. A dome-shaped lid is also useful, as is a metal draining rack that fits over the wok. Small items such as deep-fried foods can be placed on the rack to keep warm while more batches are cooked. Other useful accessories include chopsticks and a wok stand, which will help to protect your table when serving.

Strainers

The two most useful types of strainer are the perforated metal scoop or slotted spoon, and the coarse-mesh, wire skimmer, preferably with a long bamboo handle. Wire skimmers come in a variety of sizes and are useful for removing food from oil when deep-frying.

Clay pot

This earthenware cooking utensil is available in several shapes and sizes. It can be used on top of the stove, where it will retain an even heat as the food cooks.

Rice cooker

Electric rice cookers are very well designed and are worth investing in if you cook a lot of rice. However, a deep, heavy-based pan with a tight-fitting lid will make a perfectly adequate substitute.

conduct and retain heat evenly, and because of its shape, the food always returns to the centre where the heat is most intense. This makes it ideally suited for stir-frying, braising, steaming, boiling and even for deep-frying.

There are two basic types of wok available. The most common type, the double-handled wok, is suitable for all types of cooking. The single-handled wok is particularly suitable for quick stir-frying, as it can easily be shaken. Both types are available with flattened bases for use on electric or gas stoves. Choose a wok made from lightweight carbonized steel; cast iron woks are too heavy for comfort, and woks made from other materials are not suitable for the South-east Asian style of cooking.

A new wok must be seasoned before use. To do this, place it over a high heat until the surface blackens, then wash it in warm, soapy water. Use a stiff brush to get the wok clean, then rinse it in clean water and place it over a medium heat to dry. Finally, wipe the surface with kitchen paper soaked in

THAILAND, BURMA AND VIETNAM

To eat a Thai meal is an experience in itself, with subtle spice blends and exquisite flavours. Burmese food is more robust yet equally exciting, while Vietnamese cuisine shows the influence of neighbouring China, and there is evidence of traditions left over from French colonial rule.

BURMESE-STYLE PORK CURRY

The cuisine of Burma is influenced by its two neighbours, China and India. Soy sauce and noodles are obviously the result of a Chinese influence, but curry itself is definitely an Indian invention. Burmese curries are, however, much lighter.

SERVES 4–6

2.5cm/1in piece fresh root ginger, crushed
8 dried red chillies, soaked in warm water for 20 minutes
2 lemon grass stalks, finely chopped
15ml/1 tbsp chopped galangal or chopped fresh root ginger
15ml/1 tbsp shrimp paste
30ml/2 tbsp brown sugar
675g/1½lb pork, with some of its fat
600ml/1 pint/2½ cups water
10ml/2 tsp ground turmeric
5ml/1 tsp dark soy sauce
4 shallots, finely chopped
15ml/1 tbsp chopped garlic
45ml/3 tbsp tamarind juice or 5ml/1 tsp concentrated tamarind pulp
5ml/1 tsp granulated sugar
15ml/1 tbsp fish sauce
fresh red chillies, to garnish
French (green) beans, to serve

1 In a mortar, pound the ginger, chillies, lemon grass and galangal into a coarse paste with a pestle, then add the shrimp paste and brown sugar to produce a dark, grainy purée.

2 Cut the pork into large chunks and place in a wok or large pan. Add the curry purée and stir well to make sure the meat is well coated.

3 Cook the pork over a low heat, stirring occasionally, until the meat has changed colour and rendered some of its fat, and the curry paste has begun to release its aroma.

4 Stir the water, turmeric and soy sauce into the meat in the pan. Simmer gently for about 40 minutes, until the meat is tender. The pan does not need to be kept covered.

5 Add the shallots, garlic, tamarind juice, sugar and fish sauce. If you are using concentrated tamarind pulp, stir until dissolved. Garnish with fresh chillies and serve with French beans.

CHICKEN with GINGER and LEMON GRASS

This quick and easy recipe from Vietnam contains the unusual combination of ginger and lemon grass with mandarin orange and chillies. The dish is served topped with peanuts, which are first roasted, then skinned.

SERVES 4–6

3 chicken legs (thighs and drumsticks)
15ml/1 tbsp vegetable oil
2cm/¾in piece fresh root ginger,
    finely chopped
1 garlic clove, crushed
1 small fresh red chilli, seeded and
    finely chopped
5cm/2in piece lemon grass, shredded
150ml/¼ pint/⅔ cup chicken stock
15ml/1 tbsp fish sauce
10ml/2 tsp granulated sugar
2.5ml/½ tsp salt
juice of ½ lemon
50g/2oz raw peanuts
2 spring onions (scallions),
    shredded
zest of 1 mandarin or satsuma,
    shredded
plain boiled rice or rice noodles, to serve

3 To prepare the peanuts, the red skin must be removed. To do this grill (broil) or roast the peanuts under a medium heat until evenly brown, for 2–3 minutes. Turn the nuts out on to a clean cloth and rub briskly to loosen the skins.

4 Transfer the chicken from the pan to a warmed serving dish, and sprinkle with the roasted peanuts, shredded spring onions and the zest of the mandarin or satsuma. Serve hot with plain boiled rice or rice noodles.

1 With the heel of a knife, chop through the narrow end of each of the chicken drumsticks. Remove the jointed parts of the chicken, then remove the skin. Rinse and pat dry with kitchen paper.

2 Heat the oil in a wok or large pan. Add the chicken, ginger, garlic, chilli and lemon grass and cook for 3–4 minutes. Add the chicken stock, fish sauce, sugar, salt and lemon juice. Cover the pan and simmer for 30–35 minutes.

COOK'S TIP
To save yourself time and effort, buy ready-roasted peanuts. These are now available with reduced sodium for a low-salt alternative.

RED CHICKEN CURRY with BAMBOO SHOOTS

Bamboo shoots have a lovely crunchy texture. Try to buy canned whole shoots, which are crisper and of better quality than sliced shoots. It is essential to use chicken breast meat rather than any other cut for this Thai curry, as it is cooked very quickly.

SERVES 4–6

1 litre/1¾ pints/4 cups coconut milk
30ml/2 tbsp red curry paste
450g/1lb chicken breast fillets, skinned
    and cut into bitesize pieces
30ml/2 tbsp Thai fish sauce
15ml/1 tbsp granulated sugar
225g/8oz canned bamboo shoots, rinsed,
    drained and sliced
5 kaffir lime leaves, torn
salt and ground black pepper
chopped fresh red chillies and kaffir
    lime leaves, to garnish
plain boiled rice, to serve

1 Pour half of the coconut milk into a wok or large pan over a medium heat. Bring the coconut milk to the boil, stirring constantly until it has separated.

2 Add the red curry paste and cook the mixture for 2–3 minutes. Stir the paste all the time to prevent it sticking to the base of the pan.

3 Add the chicken pieces, fish sauce and sugar to the pan. Stir well, then cook for 5–6 minutes until the chicken changes colour and is cooked through. Continue to stir to prevent the mixture from sticking to the base of the pan.

4 Pour the remaining coconut milk into the pan, then add the sliced bamboo shoots and torn kaffir lime leaves. Bring back to the boil over a medium heat, stirring constantly to prevent the mixture from sticking, then taste and add salt and pepper if necessary.

5 To serve, spoon the curry into a warmed serving dish and garnish with chopped chillies and kaffir lime leaves.

VARIATION
Instead of, or as well as, bamboo shoots use green beans. Cook 115g/4oz green beans in lightly salted water for 5 minutes, then drain and stir into the curry at the end of the recipe.

BEEF CURRY in SWEET PEANUT SAUCE

The consistency of this curry is quite thick, unlike most other Thai curries. Roasted and ground peanuts add a rich taste, and thicken the sauce at the same time. You can grind the peanuts in a coffee grinder or use a pestle and mortar. For a quick alternative, you could use peanut butter, but you will need to reduce the quantity of salt.

SERVES 4–6

600ml/1 pint/2½ cups coconut milk
45ml/3 tbsp red curry paste
45ml/3 tbsp Thai fish sauce
30ml/2 tbsp palm sugar or soft light
   brown sugar
2 lemon grass stalks, bruised
450g/1lb rump steak cut into thin strips
75g/3oz roasted ground peanuts
2 fresh red chillies, sliced
5 kaffir lime leaves, torn
salt and ground black pepper
10–15 Thai basil leaves, to garnish
2 salted eggs, to serve

1 Put half the coconut milk into a wok or large pan. Heat the milk gently, stirring constantly, until it begins to boil and separate.

2 Add the red curry paste and cook over a medium heat until fragrant. Add the fish sauce, palm or light brown sugar and lemon grass.

3 Continue to cook until the colour of the curry sauce deepens.

4 Add the remaining coconut milk and bring back to the boil. Add the beef and ground peanuts. Cook for 8–10 minutes.

5 Add the sliced chillies and torn kaffir lime leaves and adjust the seasoning. Garnish with the whole Thai basil leaves, and serve with salted eggs, if you like.

GREEN BEEF CURRY with THAI AUBERGINE

Thai cuisine is packed with sensational yet perfectly balanced flavours. This dish, which is cooked in the well-known green curry paste, creates a taste explosion. Thai aubergines are much smaller than the large, purple variety sold in Western supermarkets. You can buy small aubergines from Asian stores or, alternatively, use baby aubergines.

SERVES 4–6

15ml/1 tbsp vegetable oil
45ml/3 tbsp green curry paste
600ml/1 pint/2½ cups coconut milk
450g/1lb beef sirloin
4 kaffir lime leaves, torn
15–30ml/1–2 tbsp Thai fish sauce
5ml/1 tsp palm sugar or soft light
    brown sugar
150g/5oz small Thai aubergines
    (eggplant) or baby aubergines,
    halved
2 fresh green chillies and a small handful
    of Thai basil, to garnish
plain boiled rice or noodles, to serve

1 Heat the oil in a wok or large pan. Add the green curry paste and fry gently until the paste begins to release its fragrant aromas.

2 Stir in half the coconut milk, a little at a time. Cook over a medium heat for about 5–6 minutes, until the oil begins to separate and an oily sheen appears on the surface.

3 Cut the beef into long thin slices and add to the pan with the kaffir lime leaves, fish sauce, sugar and aubergines. Cook for 2–3 minutes, then stir in the remaining coconut milk.

4 Bring back to a simmer and cook until the meat and aubergines are tender. Finely shred the green chillies and use to garnish the curry, along with the Thai basil leaves.

MUSSAMAN CURRY

Unlike its neighbouring countries, Thailand managed to remain free from colonization by European powers. As a result, its food has no outside influence, although the Thais have borrowed cooking styles from other countries, such as India and China. Mussaman Curry is one such example, which originated within the Muslim community in India.

SERVES 4–6

600ml/1 pint/2½ cups coconut milk (see Cook's Tip)
675g/1½lb stewing beef, cut into 2.cm/1in chunks
250ml/8fl oz/1 cup coconut cream
45ml/3 tbsp mussaman curry paste
30ml/2 tbsp Thai fish sauce
15ml/1 tbsp palm sugar or soft light brown sugar
60ml/4 tbsp tamarind juice or concentrated tamarind pulp
6 cardamom pods
2.5cm/1in piece cinnamon stick
225g/8oz potatoes, cut into even-size chunks
1 onion, cut into wedges
50g/2oz/⅓ cup roasted peanuts
plain boiled rice, to serve

1 Bring the coconut milk to a gentle boil in a wok or large pan. Add the beef and simmer for 40 minutes, until tender.

2 Pour the coconut cream into a small pan, then cook for 5–8 minutes, stirring constantly, until an oily sheen appears on the surface. Add the Thai mussaman curry paste and cook until fragrant.

3 Stir the curry paste into the beef. Add the fish sauce, sugar, tamarind, cardamom pods, cinnamon stick, potatoes and onions. Simmer gently for 10–15 minutes. Add the peanuts and cook for a further 5 minutes. Serve with plain boiled rice.

COOK'S TIP
Coconut milk can be made at home from desiccated (dry, unsweetened, shredded) coconut. In a food processor, process 225g/8oz/2⅔ cups desiccated coconut with 450ml/¾ pint/scant 2 cups boiling water for 20–30 seconds. Allow to cool, then ladle into a sieve (strainer) lined with muslin (cheesecloth) set over a bowl. Bring up the ends of the cloth and twist to extract the liquid. Discard the spent coconut and use the milk as directed in recipes. Unused milk will keep in the refrigerator for 1–2 days.

BURMESE FISH STEW

Housewives in Burma buy this well-known and delicious one-course meal, known as Mohingha, from hawkers, who can be recognized by a bamboo pole carried across their shoulders. At one end of the pole is a container with a charcoal fire and at the other end is everything else they need to make the meal.

SERVES 8

675g/1½lb huss, cod or mackerel,
    cleaned but left on the bone
3 lemon grass stalks
2.5cm/1in piece fresh root ginger
30ml/2 tbsp fish sauce
3 onions, roughly chopped
4 garlic cloves, roughly chopped
2–3 fresh red chillies, seeded and chopped
5ml/1 tsp ground turmeric
75ml/5 tbsp groundnut (peanut) oil,
    for frying
400g/14oz can coconut milk
25g/1oz/¼ cup rice flour
25g/1oz/¼ cup gram flour (besan)
540g/1lb/5oz canned bamboo shoots,
    rinsed, drained and sliced
salt and ground black pepper
wedges of hard-boiled (hard-cooked) egg,
    thinly sliced red onions, finely chopped
    spring onions (scallions), deep-fried
    prawns (shrimp) and fried chillies,
    to garnish
rice noodles, to serve

1 Place the fish in a large pan and pour in cold water to cover. Bruise two lemon grass stalks and half the peeled fresh root ginger and add to the pan. Bring to the boil, add the fish sauce and cook for 10 minutes. Lift out the fish with a slotted spoon, and allow to cool. Meanwhile, strain the stock into a large bowl. Discard any skin and bones from the fish and break the flesh into small pieces, using a fork.

2 Cut off the lower 5cm/2in of the remaining lemon grass stalk and discard; roughly chop the remaining lemon grass. Put it in a food processor or blender, along with the remaining ginger, the onions, garlic, chillies and turmeric. Process to a smooth paste. Heat the oil in a wok or large pan, and fry the paste until it gives off a rich, fragrant aroma. Remove the pan from the heat and add the fish pieces.

3 Stir the coconut milk into the reserved fish stock and pour into a large pan. Add water to make up to 2.5 litres/4 pints/ 10 cups. In a jug (pitcher), mix the rice flour and gram flour (besan) to a thin cream with some of the stock. Stir into the mixture. Bring to the boil, stirring.

4 Add the bamboo shoots to the pan and cook for 10 minutes until tender. Stir in the fish mixture, season to taste, and cook until heated through. Guests pour the soup over the noodles, and add hard-boiled egg, onions, spring onions, prawns and chillies as a garnish.

GREEN PRAWN CURRY

Green Curry has become a firm favourite in the West, and this prawn dish is just one of a range of delicious green curry recipes. Home-made green curry paste has the best flavour, but you can also buy it ready-made from good supermarkets.

SERVES 4–6

30ml/2 tbsp vegetable oil
30ml/2 tbsp green curry paste
450g/1lb raw king prawns (jumbo shrimp),
 peeled and deveined
4 kaffir lime leaves, torn
1 lemon grass stalk, bruised and chopped
250ml/8fl oz/1 cup coconut milk
30ml/2 tbsp fish sauce
½ cucumber, seeded and cut into
 thin batons
10–15 basil leaves
4 fresh green chillies, sliced, to garnish

1 Heat the oil in a wok or large pan. Add the green curry paste and fry gently until bubbling and fragrant.

2 Add the prawns, kaffir lime leaves and chopped lemon grass. Fry for 2 minutes, until the prawns are pink.

3 Stir in the coconut milk and bring to a gentle boil. Simmer, stirring occasionally, for about 5 minutes or until the prawns are tender.

4 Stir in the fish sauce, cucumber batons and whole basil leaves, then top with the green chillies and serve from the pan.

VARIATION
Strips of skinned chicken breast fillet can be used in place of the prawns if you prefer. Add them to the pan in step 2 and fry until browned on all sides.

PRAWNS with YELLOW CURRY PASTE

Fish and shellfish, such as prawns, and coconut milk were made for each other. This is a very quick recipe if you make the yellow curry paste in advance, or buy it ready-made. It keeps well in a screw-top jar in the refrigerator for up to four weeks.

SERVES 4–6

600ml/1 pint/2½ cups coconut milk
30ml/2 tbsp yellow curry paste
15ml/1 tbsp fish sauce
2.5ml/½ tsp salt
5ml/1 tsp granulated sugar
450g/1lb raw king prawns
    (jumbo shrimp), thawed if frozen,
    peeled and deveined
225g/8oz cherry tomatoes
juice of ½ lime
red (bell) peppers, seeded and cut into
    thin strips, and fresh coriander
    (cilantro) leaves, to garnish
plain boiled rice or rice noodles,
    to serve

1 Put half the coconut milk in a wok or large pan and bring to the boil. Add the yellow curry paste, and stir until it disperses. Lower the heat and simmer gently for about 10 minutes.

2 Add the fish sauce, salt, sugar and remaining coconut milk to the sauce. Simmer for 5 minutes more.

3 Add the prawns and cherry tomatoes. Simmer very gently for about 5 minutes until the prawns are pink and tender.

4 Spoon into a serving dish, sprinkle with lime juice and garnish with strips of pepper and coriander.

VARIATION
Use cooked prawns if preferred. Add in step 3 and heat through.

COOK'S TIP
• Unused coconut milk can be stored in the refrigerator for 1–2 days, or poured into a freezer container and frozen.
• If making your own coconut milk, instead of discarding the spent coconut, it can be reused to make a second batch of coconut milk. This will be of a poorer quality and should only be used to extend a good quality first quantity of milk.
• Leave newly made coconut milk to stand for 10 minutes. The coconut cream will float to the top: skim off with a spoon.

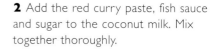 *VERY GOOD / EASY*

BEANCURD and GREEN BEAN CURRY

These days, beancurd is widely available from supermarkets and Asian stores. It has a silky appearance and an extremely soft texture. Tofu makes an excellent substitute; like beancurd, tofu is made of soya bean paste, but is much firmer. It is also much more easily available and can be found in most supermarkets and health food stores.

SERVES 4–6

600ml/1 pint/2½ cups coconut milk
15ml/1 tbsp red curry paste
45ml/3 tbsp Thai fish sauce
10ml/2 tsp palm sugar or soft light
   brown sugar
225g/8oz button (white) mushrooms
115g/4oz French (green) beans, trimmed
175g/6oz beancurd, rinsed and cut into
   2cm/¾in cubes
4 kaffir lime leaves, torn
2 fresh red chillies, sliced
fresh coriander (cilantro) sprigs, to garnish

½ fresh Chilli only →

1 Put about one-third of the coconut milk in a wok or large pan. Cook until an oily sheen appears on the surface.

2 Add the red curry paste, fish sauce and sugar to the coconut milk. Mix together thoroughly.

3 Add the button mushrooms. Stir well and cook over a medium heat for about 1 minute. Stir in the rest of the coconut milk and bring back to the boil.

4 Add the French beans and cubes of beancurd and allow to simmer gently for another 4–5 minutes.

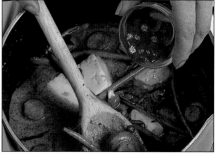

5 Stir in the kaffir lime leaves and red chillies. Serve garnished with the fresh coriander sprigs.

GREEN PAPAYA SALAD

*This salad appears in many guises in South-east Asia. If green papaya is not easy to get
hold of, finely grated carrots, cucumber or green apple can be used instead. Alternatively,
use very thinly sliced white cabbage.*

SERVES 4

1 green papaya
4 garlic cloves, roughly chopped
15ml/1 tbsp chopped shallots
3–4 fresh red chillies, seeded and sliced
2.5ml/½ tsp salt
2–3 snake beans or 6 green beans
2 tomatoes, seeded and cut into very
    thin wedges
45ml/3 tbsp Thai fish sauce
15ml/1 tbsp granulated sugar
juice of 1 lime
30ml/2 tbsp coarsely crushed
    roasted peanuts
1 fresh red chilli, seeded and sliced,
    to garnish

1 Cut the papaya in half lengthwise.
Scrape out the seeds with a spoon, then
peel using a vegetable peeler or a small
sharp knife. Shred the flesh finely using
a food processor grater.

2 Put the garlic, shallots, chillies and salt
in a large mortar and grind to a rough
paste with a pestle. Add the shredded
papaya, a little at a time, pounding until
it becomes slightly limp and soft.

3 Cut the snake beans or green beans
into 2cm/¾in lengths. Add the sliced
beans and the wedges of tomato to the
mortar and crush them very lightly with
the pestle.

4 Season the mixture with the Thai fish
sauce, sugar and lime juice. Transfer the
salad to a serving dish and sprinkle with
the crushed peanuts. Garnish with slices
of red chilli and serve.

MALAYSIA

The food of Malaysia is a rich blend of some of the world's most exciting cuisines: Malay, Chinese and Indian. The result is a harmonious mixture of flavours, some cool and some famously hot and spicy, such as the dishes cooked in the traditional style known as Nonya.

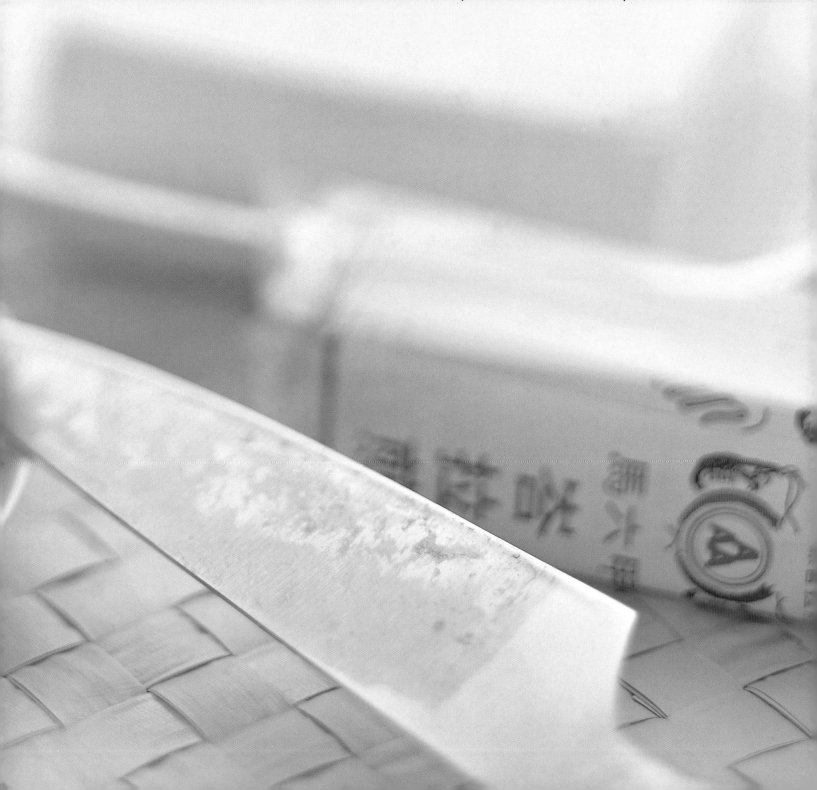

CHICKEN with SPICES and SOY SAUCE

This simple but delicious dish, known as ayam kecap, *suggests a Chinese influence.*
Although a significant number of people from China had already settled in Malaysia,
by the 15th century Malacca was established as one of the important trading posts
in the world, and more Chinese poured into the area. Together with the local Malay
people, they developed a unique style of cuisine known as Nonya.

SERVES 4

1.3–1.6kg/3–3½lb chicken, jointed and
   cut into 16 pieces
3 onions, sliced
about 1 litre/1¾ pints/4 cups water
3 garlic cloves, crushed
3–4 fresh red chillies, seeded and sliced,
   or 15ml/1 tbsp chilli powder
45ml/3 tbsp vegetable oil
2.5ml/½ tsp grated nutmeg
6 whole cloves
5ml/1 tsp tamarind pulp, soaked in 45ml/
   3 tbsp warm water
30–45ml/2–3 tbsp dark or light soy sauce
salt
fresh green and red chilli shreds, to garnish
plain boiled rice, to serve

1 Place the prepared chicken pieces in a large pan with one of the sliced onions. Pour over enough water to just cover. Bring to the boil and then reduce the heat and allow to simmer gently for about 20 minutes.

2 Grind the remaining onions, with the garlic and chillies or chilli powder, to a fine paste in a food processor or with a pestle and mortar. Heat a little of the oil in a wok or frying pan and cook the paste to bring out the flavour. Do not allow the paste to brown.

COOK'S TIP
When adding salt, start with a very small quantity and taste before adding more.

3 When the chicken has cooked for 20 minutes, lift it out of the stock and into the spicy mixture. Toss everything together over a fairly high heat so that the spices permeate the chicken pieces. Reserve 300ml/½ pint/1¼ cups of the chicken stock to add to the pan later.

4 Stir in the nutmeg and cloves. Strain the tamarind and add the tamarind juice and the soy sauce to the chicken. Cook for a further 2–3 minutes, then add the reserved stock.

5 Taste and adjust the seasoning to taste and cook, uncovered, for a further 25–35 minutes, or until the chicken pieces are tender.

6 Transfer the chicken to a bowl, topped with shredded green and red chillies, and serve with plain boiled rice.

COOK'S TIP
Dark soy sauce is thicker and more salty than light. Adding the dark variety will give a deeper colour to the chicken.

CHICKEN with GOLDEN TURMERIC

As turmeric grows abundantly throughout South-east Asia, using it fresh is quite natural for the local people. The fresh version, which is a root like ginger, has a completely different taste and produces a luxurious golden colour in a dish. It is a difficult ingredient to find in the West. A little more than the normal amount of dried ground turmeric will produce an acceptable colour, although the flavour will be somewhat different.

SERVES 4

1.3–1.6kg/3–3½lb chicken, cut into
    8 pieces, or 4 chicken quarters, halved
15ml/1 tbsp light brown sugar
3 macadamia nuts or 6 almonds
2 garlic cloves, crushed
1 large onion, quartered
2.5cm/1in piece fresh galangal or
    1cm/½in piece fresh root ginger, sliced,
    or 5ml/1 tsp galangal powder
1–2 lemon grass stalks, lower 5cm/2in
    sliced, top bruised
1cm/½in cube shrimp paste
4cm/1½in piece fresh turmeric, sliced,
    or 10ml/2 tsp ground turmeric
15ml/1 tbsp tamarind pulp, soaked in
    150ml/¼ pint/⅔ cup warm water
60–90ml/4–6 tbsp vegetable oil
400g/14oz can coconut milk
salt and ground black pepper
Deep-fried Onions, to garnish

1 Rub each of the chicken joints with a little sugar and set them aside.

2 Grind the nuts and garlic in a food processor with the onion, galangal or ginger, sliced lemon grass, shrimp paste and turmeric. Alternatively, pound the ingredients to a paste with a pestle and mortar. Strain the tamarind pulp and reserve the juice.

COOK'S TIP

In step 3, start with a medium heat and reduce it to low after 1 minute.

3 Heat the oil in a wok or large pan, and cook the paste, without browning, until it gives off a spicy aroma. Add the pieces of chicken and toss well in the spices. Add the strained tamarind juice. Spoon the coconut cream off the top of the milk and set it to one side.

4 Add the coconut milk to the pan. Cover and cook for 45 minutes, or until the chicken is tender.

5 Before serving, stir in the coconut cream. Season to taste and serve, garnished with Deep-fried Onions.

SPICED CHICKEN SAUTE

This makes a wonderfully simple supper dish. If you wish to prepare it in advance, bake the chicken and make the sauce following the recipe, then allow to cool, and store in the refrigerator until needed.

SERVES 4

1.3–1.6kg/3–3½lb chicken breast fillets,
    skinned and cut into in 8 pieces
5ml/1 tsp each salt and ground black
    pepper
2 garlic cloves, crushed
150ml/¼ pint/⅔ cup vegetable oil

For the sauce
25g/1 oz butter
30ml/2 tbsp vegetable oil
1 onion, sliced
4 garlic cloves, crushed
2 large, ripe beefsteak tomatoes, chopped
600ml/1 pint/2½ cups water
50ml/2fl oz/¼ cup dark soy sauce
salt and ground black pepper
fresh red chilli, sliced, and Deep-fried
    Onions, to garnish
plain boiled rice, to serve

1 Preheat the oven to 190°C/375°F/ Gas 5. Make two slashes in each chicken piece and rub with salt, pepper and garlic. Drizzle with oil and bake for about 30 minutes, until browned.

2 To make the sauce, heat the butter and oil and fry the onion and garlic. Add the tomatoes, water, soy sauce and seasoning. Boil for 5 minutes to reduce.

3 Add the chicken pieces to the sauce in the wok, turning the pieces over to coat them well. Continue cooking slowly for about 20 minutes until the chicken is tender. Stir the mixture occasionally.

4 Arrange the chicken on a serving platter and garnish with the chilli and Deep-fried Onions. This dish is usually served with plain boiled rice.

STIR-FRIED CHICKEN with PINEAPPLE

In this Indonesian-influenced dish, chicken fillets benefit from the wonderful tenderizing qualities of pineapple. If you use dark soy sauce, which is quite salty, use only a sprinkling of salt. A dash of sugar will achieve the flavour imparted by the local kecap manis.

SERVES 4–6

500g/1¼lb chicken breast fillets, skinned
    and thinly sliced at an angle
30ml/2 tbsp cornflour (cornstarch)
60ml/4 tbsp vegetable oil
1 garlic clove, crushed
5cm/2in piece fresh root ginger,
    cut into thin batons
1 small onion, thinly sliced
1 fresh pineapple, peeled, cored and
    cubed, or 400g/14oz can pineapple
    chunks in natural juice
30ml/2 tbsp dark soy sauce or
    15ml/1 tbsp kecap manis
1 bunch spring onions (scallions), white
    bulbs left whole, green tops sliced
salt and ground black pepper
plain boiled rice or noodles, to serve

1 Toss the strips of chicken in the cornflour with a little seasoning. Fry in hot oil until tender.

2 Lift the chicken strips out of the wok or frying pan and keep warm. Reheat the oil and fry the garlic, ginger and onion until soft, but not browned. Add the fresh pineapple and 120ml/4fl oz/ ½ cup water, or the canned pineapple pieces together with their juice.

3 Stir in the soy sauce or kecap manis and return the chicken to the pan to heat through.

4 Taste the chicken and adjust the seasoning. Stir in the whole spring onion bulbs and half the sliced green tops. Toss well together and then turn the chicken stir-fry on to a serving platter. Garnish with the remaining sliced green spring onions. Serve with plain rice or noodles.

CLAY-POT CHICKEN

This deliciously spiced dish is a refined version of the ancient cooking method, whereby the food was placed in a clay pot and buried in the dying embers of an open fire. Today, it is cooked in a low oven and the gentle heat is evenly distributed and retained by the clay pot, resulting in tender meat that melts in the mouth.

SERVES 4–6

1 × 1.3–1.6kg/3–3½lb oven-ready chicken
45ml/3 tbsp grated fresh coconut
30ml/2 tbsp vegetable oil
2 shallots or 1 small onion, finely chopped
2 garlic cloves, crushed
5cm/2in piece lemon grass
2.5cm/1in piece fresh galangal or fresh
    root ginger, thinly sliced
2 fresh green chillies, seeded and chopped
12mm/½in cube shrimp paste
400g/14oz can coconut milk
300ml/½ pint/1¼ cups chicken stock
2 kaffir lime leaves (optional)
15ml/1 tbsp granulated sugar
15ml/1 tbsp rice or white wine vinegar
2 ripe tomatoes
30ml/2 tbsp chopped fresh coriander
    leaves (cilantro), to garnish

1 To joint the chicken, remove the legs and wings with a sharp knife. Skin the pieces, divide the drumsticks from the thighs and, using kitchen scissors, remove the lower part of the chicken, leaving only the breast piece. Remove as many of the bones as you can, to make the dish easier to eat. Cut the breast piece into four or six and set aside.

2 Dry-fry the coconut in a large wok until evenly browned. Add the vegetable oil, shallots or onion, garlic, lemon grass, galangal or ginger, chillies and shrimp paste. Fry for 2–4 minutes to release the flavours. Preheat the oven to 180°C/350°F/Gas 4. Add the chicken joints to the wok and brown evenly with the spices for 2–3 minutes.

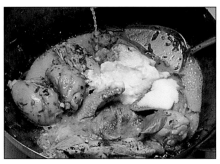

3 Strain the coconut milk, and add the thin part with the chicken stock, lime leaves, if using, sugar and vinegar. Transfer to a glazed clay pot, cover and bake in the centre of the oven for 50 minutes, or until the chicken is tender. Stir in the thick part of the coconut milk and return to the oven for 5–10 minutes.

4 Place the tomatoes in a bowl and cover with boiling water to loosen and remove the skins. Halve the tomatoes, then remove the seeds and chop into large dice. Add the chopped tomatoes to the finished dish, sprinkle with the chopped coriander and serve. Plain rice would make a good accompaniment.

BEEF and AUBERGINE CURRY

The flavour of this versatile dish is subtle yet complex. As well as the fine combination of beef and aubergine, the dish successfully unites the mellow flavour of coconut milk with the pungency of fresh chillies, and the flavours of lemon grass and tamarind. The result is a dish that is equally suitable for a family meal or a dinner party.

SERVES 6

120ml/4fl oz/½ cup vegetable oil
2 onions, thinly sliced
2.5cm/1in piece fresh root ginger, sliced
    and cut into thin batons
1 garlic clove, crushed
2 fresh red chillies, seeded and finely sliced
2.5cm/1in piece fresh turmeric, crushed,
    or 5ml/1 tsp ground turmeric
1 lemon grass stalk, lower part sliced
    finely, top bruised
675g/1½lb braising steak, cut into
    even-size strips
400g/14oz can coconut milk
300ml/½ pint/1¼ cups water
1 aubergine (eggplant), sliced and
    patted dry
5ml/1 tsp tamarind pulp, soaked in 60ml/
    4 tbsp warm water
salt and ground black pepper
finely sliced fresh chilli (optional) and
    Deep-fried Onions, to garnish
plain boiled rice, to serve

1 Heat half the oil in a wok or large pan, and fry the onions, ginger and garlic until they give off a rich aroma. Add the chillies, turmeric and the lower part of the lemon grass stalk. Push the contents of the pan to one side, then turn up the heat and add the steak, stirring until the meat changes colour.

2 Add the coconut milk, water and lemon grass top, with seasoning. Cover the pan or wok and simmer gently for 1½ hours, or until the meat is tender.

3 Towards the end of the cooking time heat the remaining oil in a frying pan. Fry the aubergine slices until they are brown on both sides.

COOK'S TIP
If you want to make this curry in advance, prepare to the end of step 2, then chill and store in the refrigerator until required.

4 Add the browned aubergine slices to the beef curry and cook for a further 15 minutes. Stir gently from time to time. Strain the tamarind and stir the juice into the curry. Taste and adjust the seasoning. Put into a warm serving dish. Garnish with the sliced chilli, if using, and Deep-fried Onions, and serve with plain boiled rice.

PRAWNS and CHAYOTE in COCONUT MILK

This delicious dish features chayote, which belongs to the squash family. Widely used in South-east Asia and some parts of India, it is pear-shaped, and generally pale yellow in colour. Larger supermarkets usually sell chayote, but you can use courgettes instead.

SERVES 4

1–2 chayotes or 2–3 courgettes (zucchini)
2 fresh red chillies, seeded
1 onion, quartered
5mm/¼in piece fresh galangal or 1cm/½in
    piece fresh root ginger, sliced
1 lemon grass stalk, lower 5cm/2in sliced,
    top bruised
2.5cm/1in piece fresh turmeric or 5ml/
    1 tsp ground turmeric
200ml/7fl oz/scant 1 cup water
lemon juice, to taste
400g/14oz can coconut milk
450g/1lb cooked, peeled prawns (shrimp)
salt
fresh red chilli shreds, to garnish
plain boiled rice or noodles, to serve

1 Peel the chayotes, remove the seeds and cut into strips. If using courgettes, cut into 5cm/2in strips.

2 Grind the fresh red chillies, onion, sliced galangal or root ginger, sliced lemon grass and the turmeric to a paste in a food processor or with a pestle and mortar. Add the water to the paste mixture, with a squeeze of lemon juice and salt to taste.

3 Pour into a pan. Add the top of the lemon grass stalk. Bring to the boil and cook for 1–2 minutes. Add the chayote or courgette pieces and then cook for 2 minutes. Stir in the coconut milk. Taste and adjust the seasoning.

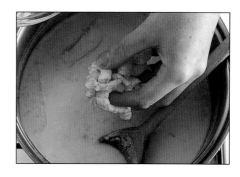

4 Add the peeled prawns and cook gently for 2–3 minutes. Remove the lemon grass stalk. Garnish with shreds of fresh red chilli, if using. This dish is usually served with plain boiled rice, but would taste equally good with rice noodles or egg noodles.

FRIED FISH with a SPICY SAUCE

Although this is not strictly a curry, it is one of the popular styles of cooking used in Malaysia. Locally known as ikan kecap, *it comes from a small range of Eurasian recipes that combine Western techniques with Eastern flavours.*

SERVES 3–4

450g/1lb fish fillets, such as mackerel,
   cod or haddock
30ml/2 tbsp plain (all-purpose) flour
groundnut (peanut) oil, for frying
1 onion, roughly chopped
1 small garlic clove, crushed
4cm/1½in piece fresh root ginger,
   grated
1–2 fresh red chillies, seeded and
   sliced
1cm/½ in cube shrimp paste, prepared
60ml/4 tbsp water
juice of ½ lemon
15ml/1 tbsp brown sugar
30ml/2 tbsp dark soy sauce
salt
roughly torn lettuce leaves, to serve

1 Rinse the fish fillets under cold water and dry on kitchen paper. Cut into serving portions and remove any bones.

2 Season the flour and use it to dust the fish. Heat some oil and fry the fish on both sides for 3–4 minutes, or until cooked. Transfer to a plate and set aside.

3 Rinse out and dry the pan. Heat a little more oil in the clean frying pan and fry the onion, garlic, ginger and chillies to bring out the flavour. Do not brown.

4 Blend the shrimp paste with the water to make a smooth paste. Add it to the onion mixture, with a little extra water if necessary. Cook for 2 minutes and then stir in the lemon juice, brown sugar and soy sauce.

5 Pour the sauce over the fish and serve, hot or cold, with roughly torn lettuce leaves.

COOK'S TIP
If serving this dish as part of a buffet menu, cut the fish into bitesize pieces.

MALAYSIAN FISH CURRY

The cooking styles of Malaysia have been greatly influenced by neighbouring countries such as India, Indonesia, China and the Middle East. The Malay people thrive on fish curry and rice. This is a superbly flavoured coconut-rich fish curry known as ikan moolee, *which is best served with a bowl of steaming hot boiled rice.*

SERVES 4

500g/1¼lb monkfish or other
    firm-textured fish fillets, skinned
    and cut into 2.5cm/1in cubes
2.5ml/½ tsp salt
50g/2oz/⅔ cup desiccated (dry,
    unsweetened, shredded) coconut
6 shallots or small onions, chopped
6 blanched almonds
2–3 garlic cloves, roughly chopped
2.5cm/1in piece fresh root ginger, sliced
2 lemon grass stalks, trimmed
10ml/2 tsp ground turmeric
45ml/3 tbsp vegetable oil
2 × 400g/14oz cans coconut milk
1–3 fresh red and green chillies, seeded
    and sliced
salt and ground black pepper, to taste
fresh chives, to garnish
plain boiled rice, to serve

1 Spread out the pieces of fish in a shallow dish and sprinkle them with the salt. Dry-fry the coconut in a wok over a gentle heat, turning all the time until it is crisp and golden (see Cook's Tip).

2 Transfer the coconut to a food processor and process to an oily paste. Scrape into a bowl and reserve.

3 Add the shallots or onions, almonds, garlic and ginger to the food processor. Cut off the lower 5cm/2in of the lemon grass stalks, chop them roughly and add to the processor. Process to a paste.

4 Add the turmeric to the mixture in the food processor and process briefly. Bruise the remaining lemon grass and set the stalks aside.

COOK'S TIP
Dry-frying is a feature of Malay cooking. When dry-frying do not be distracted. The coconut must be constantly on the move so that it becomes crisp and of a uniform golden colour.

5 Heat the oil in a wok. Add the onion mixture and cook for a few minutes without browning. Stir in the coconut milk and bring to the boil, stirring constantly to prevent curdling.

6 Add the cubes of fish to the wok, along with most of the sliced fresh chillies and the bruised lemon grass stalks. Cook for 3–4 minutes. Stir in the coconut paste (this can be moistened with some of the sauce if necessary) and cook for a further 2–3 minutes only. Do not overcook the fish. Taste the curry and adjust the seasoning, as required.

7 Remove the lemon grass. Transfer to a hot serving dish and sprinkle with the remaining slices of chilli. Garnish with chopped and whole chives and serve with plain boiled rice.

CUCUMBER and PINEAPPLE SAMBAL

Sambals are the little side dishes served at almost every Malay meal. In poorer societies, a main meal may simply be a bowl of rice and a sambal made from pounded shrimp paste, chillies and lime juice: the sambal is poured over the rice to give it flavour. This recipe is known as sambal nanas. *Use sparingly, as it is quite fiery.*

SERVES 8–10

1 small or ½ large fresh ripe pineapple
½ cucumber, halved lengthways
50g/2oz dried shrimps
1 large fresh red chilli, seeded
1.25cm/½ in cube shrimp paste, prepared
juice of 1 large lemon or lime
light brown sugar, to taste (optional)
salt

1 Cut off the top and the bottom of the pineapple. Stand it upright on a board, then slice off the skin from top to bottom, cutting out the spines. Slice the pineapple, removing the central core. Cut into thin slices and set aside.

2 Trim the ends from the cucumber and slice thinly. Sprinkle with salt and set aside. Place the dried shrimps in a food processor and chop finely. Add the chilli, prepared shrimp paste and lemon or lime juice, and process again to a paste.

3 Rinse the cucumber, drain and dry on kitchen paper. Mix the pineapple and chill. Just before serving, spoon in the spice mixture with sugar to taste, if liked. Mix well and serve.

COOK'S TIP
The pungent shrimp paste, also called blachan and terasi, is popular in many South-east Asian countries, and is available in Asian food markets. Since it can taste a bit raw in a sambal, dry fry it by wrapping it in foil and heating it in a frying pan over a low heat for 5 minutes, turning from time to time. If the shrimp paste is to be fried with other spices, this preliminary cooking can be eliminated.

INDONESIA

Numerous cultures have flourished among the 13,000 islands of this lush tropical archipelago, including the Dutch, Portuguese and British. The result is a rich culinary heritage that makes use of an abundance of indigenous ingredients, such as rice, chillies, limes, tamarind and spices.

CHICKEN COOKED in COCONUT MILK

Traditionally, the chicken pieces in this dish would be part-cooked by frying, but roasting in the oven can be a better option. This is an unusual recipe in that the sauce is white, as it does not contain chillies or turmeric, unlike many other Indonesian dishes. The dish is usually sprinkled with crisp Deep-fried Onions before serving.

SERVES 4

1.3–1.6kg/3–3½lb chicken or 4 chicken
   quarters
4 garlic cloves
1 onion, sliced
4 macadamia nuts or 8 almonds
15ml/1 tbsp coriander seeds, dry-fried,
   or 5ml/1 tsp ground coriander
45ml/3 tbsp vegetable oil
2.5cm/1in piece fresh galangal or
   4cm/1½in piece fresh root ginger,
   bruised
2 lemon grass stalks, fleshy part bruised
3 lime leaves
2 bay leaves
5ml/1 tsp granulated sugar
600ml/1 pint/2½ cups coconut milk
salt
Deep-fried Onions, to garnish
plain boiled rice, to serve

1 Preheat the oven to 190°C/375°F/ Gas 5. Cut the chicken into four or eight pieces. Season with salt. Put in an oiled roasting pan. Bake for 25–30 minutes.

COOK'S TIP
For fan assisted ovens, reduce the temperature by at least 10°C/20°F/Gas 1 when cooking the chicken in step 1. Check the chicken from time to time.

2 To make the sauce, grind the garlic, onion, nuts and coriander to a fine paste in a food processor or with a pestle and mortar. Heat the oil in a wok and lightly fry the paste to bring out the flavour.

3 Add the chicken pieces to the wok together with the galangal or ginger, lemon grass, lime and bay leaves, sugar, coconut milk and salt. Mix well.

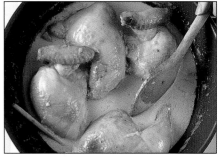

4 Bring to the boil and then reduce the heat and allow to simmer gently for 30–40 minutes, uncovered, until the chicken is tender and the coconut sauce is reduced and thickened. Stir the mixture occasionally during cooking.

5 Just before serving, remove the bruised galangal or ginger and lemon grass. Serve with plain boiled rice, sprinkled with Deep-fried Onions.

VARIATION
Instead of deep-frying the onions, coat them with oil, and bake until browned at the same time as the chicken.

MADURA CHICKEN with AROMATIC SPICES

Spices, such as the coriander and cumin used in this recipe, are added to a dish mainly for their taste. With the inclusion of nutmeg and cloves, magadip, *as it is known in Indonesia, combines both taste and aroma. It is best cooked a day or two in advance to allow the flavours to mellow and permeate the flesh of the chicken.*

SERVES 4

1.3–1.6kg/3–3½lb chicken, cut into
   quarters, or 4 chicken quarters
5ml/1 tsp granulated sugar
30ml/2 tbsp coriander seeds
10ml/2 tsp cumin seeds
6 whole cloves
2.5ml/½ tsp grated nutmeg
2.5ml/½ tsp ground turmeric
1 small onion
2.5cm/1in piece fresh root ginger,
   thinly sliced
300ml/½ pint/1¼ cups chicken stock
   or water
salt and ground black pepper
Deep-fried Onions, to garnish
plain boiled rice, to serve

1 Cut each chicken quarter in half to make eight pieces. Place the pieces in a flameproof casserole, sprinkle with the sugar and season to taste with salt and pepper. Toss the chicken pieces and seasoning together. This helps release the juices in the chicken. Use the chicken backbone and any remaining carcass, if using, to make chicken stock for use later in the recipe, if you like (see Cook's Tip).

2 In a preheated wok or large pan, dry-fry the coriander and cumin seeds and the whole cloves until the spices give off a good aroma. Add the nutmeg and turmeric and heat briefly. Remove and cool. Grind in a spice mill or food processor or use a pestle and mortar.

3 In a food processor, process the onion and ginger until finely chopped. Otherwise, finely chop the onion and ginger and pound to a paste with a pestle and mortar. Add the spices and stock or water and mix well.

4 Pour the spice mixture over the chicken in the flameproof casserole, and stir to ensure the pieces are well coated. Cover the casserole with a lid and cook over a gentle heat for 45–50 minutes until the chicken pieces are tender.

5 Serve the chicken with the sauce on plain boiled rice, sprinkled with crisp Deep-fried Onions.

COOK'S TIP
Add a large piece of bruised fresh root ginger, a small onion studded with a clove, a carrot and a stick of celery and a few peppercorns to the chicken stock to ensure a good flavour.

BEEF RENDANG with DEEP-FRIED ONIONS

In Indonesia, Rendang would be made of prime quality beef, but it can be made with other meats such as lamb, pork or even venison. The flavour of this dish improves significantly if it is cooked a day or two in advance and reheated.

SERVES 6–8

1kg/2¼lb prime beef in one piece
2 onions or 5–6 shallots, sliced
4 garlic cloves, crushed
2.5cm/1in piece fresh galangal, sliced, or
   5ml/1 tsp galangal powder
2.5cm/1in piece fresh root ginger, sliced
4–6 fresh red chillies, seeded and sliced
1 lemon grass stalk, lower part, sliced
2.5cm/1in piece fresh turmeric, sliced,
   or 5ml/1 tsp ground turmeric
5ml/1 tsp coriander seeds, dry-fried
   and ground
5ml/1 tsp cumin seeds, dry-fried
   and ground
2 lime leaves
5ml/1 tsp tamarind pulp, soaked in
   60ml/4 tbsp warm water
2 × 400g/14oz cans coconut milk
300ml/½ pint/1¼ cups water
30ml/2 tbsp dark soy sauce
8 small new potatoes, scrubbed
salt
plain boiled rice, to serve (optional)

For the deep-fried onions
450g/1lb onions
vegetable oil, for deep-frying

1 Cut the meat into long strips and then into even-size pieces. Place in a large mixing bowl and set aside.

2 Grind the onions or shallots, garlic, fresh galangal or galangal powder, ginger, chillies, sliced lemon grass and turmeric to a fine paste in a food processor or with a pestle and mortar.

3 Add the paste to the meat with the coriander and cumin and mix well. Tear the lime leaves and add them to the mixture. Cover and leave in a cool place to marinate while you prepare the rest of the ingredients.

4 Strain the tamarind and reserve the juice. Place the spiced meat and soy sauce into a wok or large pan, and stir in the coconut milk, water and tamarind juice. Season to taste with salt.

COOK'S TIPS
• If you cannot find either fresh or dried galangal (sold in Asian food stores), use extra fresh root ginger.
• Deep-fried Onions, known as Bawang Goreng, are a traditional Indonesian garnish used to accompany many dishes. They are available ready-prepared from Asian food stores. If preparing them yourself, try to find the small red onions, as they contain less water and are more suitable for this recipe.
• Deep-fried onions may be made in advance and stored in a cool, dark place in an airtight container.

5 Stir until the liquid comes to the boil and then reduce the heat and simmer gently, half-covered, for 1½–2 hours or until the meat is tender and the liquid is reduced.

6 Add the potatoes 20–25 minutes before the end of the cooking time. They will absorb some of the sauce, so add a little more water to compensate for this if you prefer the Rendang to be rather moister than it would be in Indonesia. Adjust the seasoning and keep warm.

7 To make the Deep-fried Onions, slice the onions as finely as possible, then spread out in a single layer on kitchen paper, and leave to dry in an airy place for 30 minutes–2 hours. Heat the oil in a deep-fryer or wok to 190°C/375°F. Fry the onions in batches, until crisp and golden, turning all the time. Drain on kitchen paper and allow to cool.

8 Transfer the Beef Rendang to a warmed serving bowl and sprinkle with the Deep-fried Onions. Plain boiled rice would make a good accompaniment.

GINGER-FLAVOURED DUCK with CHINESE MUSHROOMS

Ducks are often seen, comically herded in single file, along the water channels between the rice paddies throughout Indonesia. There is a substantial Chinese population in Indonesia, among whom duck is a particular favourite. The delicious ingredients in this recipe give it an unmistakable flavour.

3 Cut the slices of fresh root ginger into thin batons and fry with the onion in the duck fat, until they give off a good aroma. Set aside the ginger and onion. Lift the duck pieces out of the soy sauce marinade and transfer to the pan. Fry them until browned on both sides. Add the mushrooms and reserved liquid.

4 Add 600ml/1 pint/2½ cups of stock or water to the browned duck pieces in the pan. Add the onion and ginger and season to taste with salt and ground black pepper. Cover the pan with a lid and cook over a gentle heat for about 1 hour, until the duck is tender.

5 Slice the spring onion tops and set aside. Add the corn cobs and the white part of the spring onions and cook for a further 10 minutes. Remove from the heat and add the cornflour paste. Return to the heat and bring to the boil, stirring. Cook for 1 minute until glossy. Sprinkle with the spring onion tops, and serve with plain boiled rice.

SERVES 4

2.5kg/5½lb duck
5ml/1 tsp granulated sugar
50ml/2fl oz/¼ cup light soy sauce
2 garlic cloves, crushed
8 dried Chinese mushrooms, soaked in
    warm water for 15 minutes
5cm/2in piece fresh root ginger, sliced
1 onion, sliced
200g/7oz baby corn cobs
½ bunch spring onions (scallions)
15–30ml/1–2 tbsp cornflour (cornstarch),
    mixed with 60ml/4 tbsp water
salt and ground black pepper
plain boiled rice, to serve

1 Cut the duck along the breastbone, open it up and cut along each side of the backbone. Use the backbone, wings and giblets to make a stock to use later in the recipe. Any trimmings of fat can be rendered in a wok or large pan to use later. Cut each leg and each breast in half. Place in a bowl, rub with sugar and pour over the soy sauce and garlic.

2 Drain the mushrooms, reserving the soaking liquid. Trim, discarding the stalks.

VARIATION
Replace the corn with chopped celery and slices of canned water chestnuts.

BALINESE FISH CURRY

On the beautiful island of Bali, along with neighbouring Java and Sumatra, fish curry and rice constitute the population's dietary staples. Food here has simple, uncomplicated yet delicious flavours. Handle the fish carefully as both cod and haddock flake easily. Alternatively, use a firm-textured fish such as monkfish, swordfish or fresh tuna.

SERVES 4–6

675g/1½lb cod or haddock fillet
1cm/½in cube shrimp paste
2 red or white onions, roughly chopped
2.5cm/1in piece fresh root ginger, sliced
1cm/½in piece fresh galangal, sliced,
    or 5ml/1 tsp galangal powder
2 garlic cloves
1–2 fresh red chillies, seeded, or
    10ml/2 tsp chilli sambal,
    or 5–10ml/1–2 tsp chilli powder
90ml/6 tbsp vegetable oil
15ml/1 tbsp dark soy sauce
5ml/1 tsp tamarind pulp, soaked in
    30ml/2 tbsp warm water
250ml/8fl oz/1 cup water
celery leaves or chopped fresh chilli,
    to garnish
plain boiled rice, to serve

1 Skin the fish and remove any bones, if necessary. Cut the flesh into bitesize pieces. Pat dry with kitchen paper and set aside.

2 Grind the shrimp paste, onions, ginger, fresh galangal, if using, garlic and fresh chillies, if using, to a paste in a food processor or with a pestle and mortar. Stir in the Chilli Sambal or chilli powder and galangal powder, if using.

VARIATION
Substitute 450g/1lb cooked tiger prawns (shrimp) for the fish. Add them to the sauce 3 minutes before the end of cooking and heat through thoroughly.

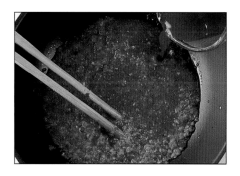

3 Heat 30ml/2 tbsp of the oil and fry the spice mixture, stirring, until it gives off a rich aroma. Add the soy sauce. Strain the tamarind and add the juice and water. Cook for 2–3 minutes.

4 In a separate pan, fry the fish in the remaining oil for 2–3 minutes. Turn once only so that the pieces stay whole. Lift out with a slotted spoon and put into the sauce.

5 Cook the fish in the sauce for a further 3 minutes. Garnish the dish with feathery celery leaves or a little chopped fresh chilli. Serve with plain boiled rice.

COOK'S TIP
Galangal paste is sold in Asian stores and can be used in place of galangal powder. It is worth buying a jar as it will keep in the refrigerator for several weeks.

SAMBAL GORENG with PRAWNS

This is an immensely useful and adaptable sauce. Here it is combined with prawns and green pepper, but you could use fine strips of calf's liver or chicken livers in place of the prawns, and tomatoes and green beans in place of the pepper.

SERVES 4–6

350g/12oz peeled cooked prawns (shrimp)
1 green (bell) pepper, seeded and
    thinly sliced
60ml/4 tbsp tamarind juice
pinch of granulated sugar
45ml/3 tbsp coconut milk or cream
lime strips and sliced red onion,
    to garnish
plain boiled rice, to serve

For the Sambal Goreng
2.5cm/1in cube shrimp paste
2 onions, roughly chopped
2 garlic cloves, roughly chopped
2.5cm/1in piece fresh galangal, sliced
2 fresh red chillies, seeded and sliced
1.5ml/¼ tsp salt
30ml/2 tbsp vegetable oil
45ml/3 tbsp tomato purée (paste)
600ml/1 pint/2½ cups vegetable stock
    or water

1 To make the Sambal Goreng, grind the shrimp paste with the onions and garlic using a mortar and pestle or a food processor. Add the galangal, chillies and salt. Pound or process to a paste.

2 Heat the oil in a wok or large pan and fry the paste for 2 minutes, without browning, until the mixture gives off a rich aroma. Stir in the tomato purée and the stock or water. Cook for 10 minutes. Ladle half the sauce into a bowl and leave to cool. This leftover sauce can be used in another recipe (see Cook's Tip).

VARIATIONS
To make Tomato Sambal Goreng, add 450g/1lb peeled, coarsely chopped tomatoes to the sauce mixture before stirring in the stock or water. To make Egg Sambal Goreng, add 3 or 4 chopped hard-boiled (hard-cooked) eggs, and 2 peeled, chopped tomatoes to the sauce.

3 Add the prawns and green pepper to the remaining sauce in the wok. Cook gently for 3–4 minutes, then stir in the tamarind juice, sugar and coconut milk or cream. Spoon into serving bowls and garnish with strips of lime rind and sliced red onion. Serve with plain boiled rice.

COOK'S TIP
Any remaining sauce can be stored in the refrigerator for up to 3 days. It can also be frozen for up to 3 months.

PRAWN CURRY with QUAIL'S EGGS

This exotic combination lives up to all the promises of the East. The earthy flavour of ginger is blended with refreshing lemon grass, fiery red chillies and soothing coconut milk to create this exquisite dish. Quail's eggs are now stocked in most supermarkets.

SERVES 4

12 quail's eggs
30ml/2 tbsp vegetable oil
4 shallots or 1 onion, finely chopped
2.5cm/1in piece fresh galangal or
   2.5cm/1in piece fresh root ginger,
   chopped
2 garlic cloves, crushed
5cm/2in piece lemon grass,
   finely shredded
1–2 small fresh red chillies, seeded and
   finely chopped
2.5ml/½ tsp ground turmeric
12mm/½in cube shrimp paste or
   15ml/1 tbsp fish sauce
900g/2lb raw prawn (shrimp) tails,
   peeled and deveined
400g/14oz can coconut milk
300ml/½ pint/1¼ cups chicken stock
115g/4oz Chinese leaves,
   roughly shredded
10ml/2 tsp granulated sugar
2.5ml/½ tsp salt
2 spring onions (scallions), green part
   only, shredded, and 30ml/2 tbsp
   shredded coconut, to garnish

1 Boil the quail's eggs for 8 minutes. Refresh in cold water, peel by dipping in cold water to release the shells and set them aside.

2 Heat the vegetable oil in a large wok, add the shallots or onion, galangal or ginger and garlic and cook until the onions have softened, without colouring. Add the lemon grass, chillies, turmeric and shrimp paste or fish sauce and fry briefly to bring out their flavours.

3 Add the prawns to the wok and fry briefly. Pour the coconut milk through a sieve (strainer) over a bowl, then add the thin part of the milk with the chicken stock. Add the Chinese leaves, sugar and salt, and bring to the boil. Simmer for 6–8 minutes.

4 Turn out the prawn curry on to a warmed serving dish. Halve the quail's eggs, using a sharp knife for a clean cut, and toss them in the sauce until they are well coated. Sprinkle with the spring onions and the shredded coconut. Serve with plain boiled rice, if you like.

SQUID in CLOVE SAUCE

The island of Madura, between Bali and Java, makes use of various spices that were originally introduced to Indonesia by Indian and Arab traders. This recipe with cloves and nutmeg, along with tomato and soy sauce, is known as Cumi Cumi Smoor. *It is quite delicious, and not difficult to make.*

SERVES 3–4

675g/1½lb ready-cleaned squid
45ml/3 tbsp groundnut (peanut) oil
1 onion, finely chopped
2 garlic cloves, crushed
1 beefsteak tomato, skinned and chopped
15ml/1 tbsp dark soy sauce
2.5ml/½ tsp grated nutmeg
6 whole cloves
150ml/¼ pint/⅔ cup water
juice of ½ lemon or lime
salt and ground black pepper, to taste
shredded spring onions (scallions) and fresh
    coriander (cilantro) sprigs, to garnish
plain boiled rice, to serve

1 Wash the squid and pat dry on kitchen paper. Use a sharp kitchen knife to cut the squid into long, thin ribbons. Carefully remove the "bone" from each tentacle, and discard.

2 Heat a wok, toss in the squid and stir constantly for 2–3 minutes, when the squid will have curled into attractive shapes or into firm rings. Lift out and set aside in a warm place.

3 Heat the oil in a clean pan and fry the onion and garlic, until soft and beginning to brown. Add the tomato, soy sauce, nutmeg, cloves, water and lemon or lime juice. Bring to the boil and then reduce the heat and add the squid, with seasoning to taste.

4 Cook the squid in the sauce for 4 minutes, uncovered, over a gentle heat, stirring from time to time. Take care not to overcook the squid. Serve hot or warm, with plain rice, or as part of a buffet spread. Garnish with shredded spring onions and fresh coriander.

VARIATION
Instead of squid try using 450g/1lb cooked and peeled tiger prawns (shrimp) in this recipe. Add them to the pan for the final 1–2 minutes.

FRUIT and RAW VEGETABLE GADO-GADO

Banana leaves, which can be bought from Asian markets, lend an authentic touch to all types of South-east Asian dishes. They are most frequently used as wrappers in which to cook small parcels of food, but if you are serving this salad for a special occasion, you could use a single banana leaf instead of the mixed salad leaves to line the platter.

SERVES 6

½ cucumber
2 pears (not too ripe) or 175g/6oz wedge
   of yam bean
1–2 eating apples
juice of ½ lemon
mixed salad leaves or 1–2 banana leaves
6 tomatoes, seeded and cut into wedges
3 fresh pineapple slices, cored and cut
   into wedges
3 eggs, hard-boiled (hard-cooked) and
   shelled
175g/6oz egg noodles, cooked, cooled
   and chopped
Deep-fried Onions, to garnish

For the peanut sauce
2–4 fresh red chillies, seeded and ground,
   or 15ml/1 tbsp Hot Tomato Sambal
300ml/½ pint/1¼ cups coconut milk
350g/12oz/1¼ cups crunchy peanut butter
15ml/1 tbsp dark soy sauce or dark brown
   sugar
5ml/1 tsp tamarind pulp, soaked in 45ml/
   3 tbsp warm water
coarsely crushed peanuts
salt

VARIATION
Quail's eggs can be used in place of hen's eggs. Hard boil for 3 minutes.

1 Make the peanut sauce. Put the ground chillies or Hot Tomato Sambal in a pan. Pour in the coconut milk, then stir in the peanut butter. Heat gently, stirring, until well blended.

2 Simmer gently until the sauce thickens, then stir in the soy sauce or sugar. Strain in the tamarind juice, add salt to taste and stir well. Spoon into a bowl and sprinkle with coarsely crushed peanuts.

3 To make the salad, core the cucumber and peel the pears or yam bean. Cut the flesh into fine matchsticks. Finely shred the apples and sprinkle them with the lemon juice. Spread a bed of mixed salad leaves on a flat platter and pile the cucumber, pear or yam bean, apple, tomato and pineapple on top.

4 Add the sliced or quartered hard-boiled eggs, the chopped noodles and garnish with the Deep-fried Onions. Serve the salad at once, with the peanut sauce.

SAMBAL KECAP, HOT TOMATO SAMBAL and CUCUMBER SAMBAL

Piquant sambals are placed on the table as a condiment for dipping meat and fish.

SAMBAL KECAP

MAKES ABOUT 150ML/¼ PINT/⅔ CUP

1 fresh red chilli, seeded and
   finely chopped
2 garlic cloves, crushed
60ml/4 tbsp dark soy sauce
20ml/4 tsp lemon juice, or
   15–25ml/1–1½ tbsp prepared tamarind
   juice or 5ml/1 tsp concentrated
   tamarind pulp
30ml/2 tbsp hot water
30ml/2 tbsp Deep-fried Onions

1 Mix the chilli, garlic, soy sauce, lemon
juice or tamarind juice or pulp and hot
water together in a bowl.

2 Stir in the Deep-fried Onions and
then leave the sambal to stand for
30 minutes before serving.

HOT TOMATO SAMBAL

MAKES 120ML/4FL OZ/½ CUP

3 ripe tomatoes
2.5ml/½ tsp salt
5ml/1 tsp chilli sauce
60ml/4 tbsp fish sauce or soy sauce
15ml/1 tbsp chopped fresh coriander
   (cilantro) leaves

1 Cover the tomatoes with boiling
water to loosen the skins. Remove the
skins, halve, discard the seeds and chop
the flesh finely.

2 Place the chopped tomatoes in a large
bowl, add the salt, chilli sauce, fish sauce
or soy sauce and chopped coriander.

3 Mix together well. Leave the sambal
to stand for 30 minutes before serving.

CUCUMBER SAMBAL

MAKES 150ML/5FL OZ/⅔ CUP

1 clove garlic, crushed
5ml/1 tsp fennel seeds
10ml/2 tsp granulated sugar
2.5ml/½ tsp salt
2 shallots or 1 small onion, finely sliced
100ml/4fl oz/½ cup rice or white wine
   vinegar
¼ cucumber, finely diced

1 Place the garlic, fennel seeds, sugar
and salt in a pestle and mortar and
pound finely. Alternatively, grind the
ingredients thoroughly in a food
processor.

2 Stir in the shallots or onion, vinegar
and cucumber. Leave to stand for 6–8
hours to allow the flavours to combine.

COCONUT and PEANUT RELISH and HOT CHILLI and GARLIC DIPPING SAUCE

These flavoursome accompaniments can be served with many Indonesian dishes.

COCONUT AND PEANUT RELISH

MAKES 120ML/4FL OZ/½ CUP

115g/4oz fresh coconut, grated,
    or desiccated (dry, unsweetened,
    shredded) coconut
175g/6oz/1 cup salted peanuts
5mm/¼in cube shrimp paste
1 small onion, quartered
2–3 garlic cloves, crushed
45ml/3 tbsp vegetable oil
2.5ml/½ tsp tamarind pulp, soaked in
    30ml/2 tbsp warm water
5ml/1 tsp coriander seeds, roasted
    and ground
2.5ml/½ tsp cumin seeds, roasted
    and ground
5ml/1 tsp dark brown sugar

1 Dry-fry the coconut in a wok or large pan over a medium heat, stirring the coconut constantly until crisp and golden colour. Allow to cool and add half to the peanuts in a bowl. Toss together to mix.

2 Process the shrimp paste, the onion and garlic in a food processor or with a pestle and mortar to form a paste. Fry the paste in hot oil, without browning.

3 Strain the tamarind and reserve the juice. Add the coriander, cumin, tamarind juice and brown sugar to the fried paste in the pan. Cook for 3 minutes, stirring.

4 Stir in the remaining toasted coconut and leave to cool. When cold, mix with the peanut and coconut mixture. Leave to stand for 30 minutes before serving.

HOT CHILLI AND GARLIC DIPPING SAUCE

MAKES 120ML/4FL OZ/½ CUP

1 garlic clove
2 fresh Thai red chillies, seeded and
    roughly chopped
10ml/2 tsp granulated sugar
5ml/1 tsp tamarind juice
60ml/4 tbsp soy sauce
juice of ½ lime

1 Process the garlic, chillies and sugar in a food processor or with a pestle and mortar to create a smooth paste.

2 Add the tamarind juice, soy sauce and lime juice, and mix together. Leave to stand for 30 minutes before serving.

THE PHILIPPINES

Filipino cuisine shows the influence of neighbouring China, Malaysia, Japan and Indonesia, but by far the strongest influence came from the Spanish settlers who arrived to colonize the islands in the 16th century, and stayed for nearly 400 years.

MIXED MEAT SOUP

A Filipino pot-au-feu with Spanish connections, this dish is known as Puchero. Sometimes it is served as two courses, first soup, then meat and vegetables with rice, but it can happily be served as is, on rice in a wide soup bowl. Either way it is very satisfying, and a siesta afterwards is highly recommended.

SERVES 6–8

225g/8oz/generous 1 cup chickpeas,
    soaked overnight in water to cover
1.3kg/3lb chicken, cut into 8 pieces
350g/12oz belly of pork, rinded, or pork
    fillet, cubed
2 chorizo, thickly sliced
2 onions, chopped
2.5 litres/4 pints/10 cups water
60ml/4 tbsp vegetable oil
2 garlic cloves, crushed
3 large tomatoes, peeled, seeded
    and chopped
15ml/1 tbsp tomato purée (paste)
1–2 sweet potatoes, cut into 1cm/
    ½in cubes
2 plantains or unripe bananas,
    sliced (optional)
salt and ground black pepper
chives or chopped spring onions
    (scallions), to garnish
½ head Chinese leaves (Chinese cabbage),
    shredded, to serve

For the aubergine sauce
1 large aubergine (eggplant)
3 garlic cloves, crushed
60–90ml/4–6 tbsp wine or cider vinegar

1 Drain the chickpeas and put them in a pan. Cover with water, bring to the boil and boil rapidly for 10 minutes. Reduce the heat and simmer for 30 minutes until the chickpeas are half tender. Drain.

2 Put the chicken pieces, pork, chorizo and half of the onions in a pan. Add the chickpeas and pour in the water. Bring to the boil and lower the heat, cover and simmer for 1 hour or until the meat is just tender when tested with a skewer.

3 Meanwhile, make the aubergine sauce. Preheat the oven to 200°C/400°F/Gas 6. Prick the aubergine in several places, then place it on a baking sheet and bake for 30 minutes or until very soft.

4 Cool slightly, then peel away the aubergine skin and scrape the flesh into a bowl. Mash the flesh with the crushed garlic, season to taste and add enough vinegar to sharpen the sauce, which should be quite piquant. Set aside.

5 Heat the oil in a wok or large pan and fry the remaining onion and garlic for 5 minutes, until soft but not brown. Add the tomatoes and tomato purée and cook for 2 minutes, then add this mixture to a pan with the diced sweet potato. Add the plantains or unripe bananas, if using. Cook over a gentle heat for 20 minutes until the sweet potato is cooked. Add the Chinese leaves for the last minute or two.

6 Spoon the thick meat soup into a soup tureen, and put the vegetables in a separate serving bowl. Garnish both with whole or chopped chives or spring onions and serve with Chinese leaves and the aubergine sauce. Plain boiled rice goes very well with this dish.

SWEET and SOUR PORK with COCONUT SAUCE

This is known as adobo *in the Philippines, which refers to a cooking style rather than the name of the dish. There are many variations of the recipe, and this version includes papaya, because the enzymes in the unripe fruit are excellent for tenderizing meat.*

SERVES 4–6

675g/1½lb lean pork, diced
1 garlic clove, crushed
5ml/1 tsp paprika
5ml/1 tsp crushed black peppercorns
15ml/1 tbsp granulated sugar
175ml/6fl oz/¾ cup palm or cider vinegar
2 small bay leaves
425ml/15fl oz/1¾ cups chicken stock
50g/2oz creamed coconut (coconut cream)
150ml/¼ pint/¾ cup vegetable oil,
    for frying
1 under-ripe papaya, peeled, seeded and
    chopped
salt
½ cucumber, peeled and cut into batons,
    2 firm tomatoes, skinned, seeded and
    chopped, and 1 small bunch chives,
    chopped, to garnish

1 Marinate the pork with the garlic, paprika, black pepper, sugar, vinegar and bay leaves in a cool place for 2 hours. Add the chicken stock and coconut.

2 Transfer to a wok and simmer gently for 30–35 minutes, then remove the pork and drain. In a frying pan, heat the oil and brown the pork. Remove and drain.

3 Return the pork to the sauce with the papaya, season with salt and simmer for 15–20 minutes. Garnish with the cucumber batons, chopped tomatoes and chives and serve.

COOK'S TIP
If creamed coconut is not available, use 50ml/2fl oz/10 tsp coconut cream.

BRAISED BEEF in a RICH PEANUT SAUCE

Like many dishes brought to the Philippines by Spanish settlers, this slow-cooking estofado, renamed kari kari, retains much of its original charm. Rice and peanuts are used to thicken the juices, yielding a rich glossy sauce.

SERVES 4–6

900g/2lb stewing beef, chuck, shin
   or blade steak
30ml/2 tbsp vegetable oil
15ml/1 tbsp annatto seeds, or 5ml/1 tsp
   paprika and a pinch of ground turmeric
2 onions, chopped
2 garlic cloves, crushed
275g/10oz celeriac or swede (rutabaga),
   peeled and roughly chopped
425ml/15fl oz/1¾ cups beef stock
350g/12oz new potatoes, peeled and
   cut into large dice
15ml/1 tbsp fish sauce
30ml/2 tbsp tamarind sauce
10ml/2 tsp granulated sugar
1 bay leaf
1 sprig thyme
45ml/3 tbsp long grain rice
50g/2oz/⅓ cup peanuts or 30ml/2 tbsp
   peanut butter
15ml/1 tbsp white wine vinegar
salt and ground black pepper

1 Cut the beef into 2.5cm/1in cubes and set aside.

2 Heat the vegetable oil in a wok or large pan. Add the annatto seeds, if using, and stir to colour the oil a dark red. Remove the seeds with a slotted spoon and discard. If you are not using annatto seeds, paprika and turmeric can be added later.

3 Soften the onions, garlic and the celeriac or swede in the oil without letting them colour. Add the beef cubes and fry over a high heat to seal. If you are not using annatto seeds to redden the sauce, stir in the paprika and ground turmeric with the beef.

4 Add the beef stock, potatoes, fish sauce and tamarind sauce, granulated sugar, bay leaf and thyme. Bring to a simmer and allow to cook on the top of the stove for about 2 hours.

5 Cover the rice with cold water and leave to stand for 30 minutes. Roast the peanuts under a hot grill (broiler), if using, then rub the skins off in a clean cloth. Drain the rice and grind with the peanuts or peanut butter, using a pestle and mortar, or food processor.

6 When the beef is tender, add 60ml/ 4 tbsp of the cooking liquid to the ground rice and nuts. Blend smoothly and stir into the contents of the pan. Simmer gently on the stove to thicken, for about 15–20 minutes. To finish, stir in the wine vinegar and season well.

FISH in SPICED VINEGAR

This fish dish, cooked in the pickling style, is served hot and is known as escabeche. *It is eaten wherever there are or have been Spanish settlers. In the Philippines, palm vinegar is commonly used as a souring agent, but herb or cider vinegars will work just as well.*

SERVES 6

675–900g/1½–2lb white fish fillets,
    such as sole, plaice or flounder
45–60ml/3–4 tbsp seasoned flour
vegetable oil, for shallow frying

For the sauce
30ml/2 tbsp vegetable oil
2.5cm/1in piece fresh root ginger,
    thinly sliced
2–3 garlic cloves, crushed
1 onion, cut into thin rings
½ large green (bell) pepper, seeded and
    cut into small neat squares
½ large red (bell) pepper, seeded and
    cut into small neat squares
1 carrot, cut into thin batons
25ml/1½ tbsp cornflour (cornstarch)
450ml/¾ pint/scant 2 cups water
45–60ml/3–4 tbsp herb or cider vinegar
15ml/1 tbsp light soft brown sugar
5–10ml/1–2 tsp fish sauce
salt and ground black pepper
1 small fresh chilli, seeded and sliced and
    spring onions (scallions), finely
    shredded, to garnish
plain boiled rice, to serve

1 Wipe the fish fillets and leave them whole, or cut into serving portions, if you like. Pat dry on kitchen paper then dust lightly with the seasoned flour.

2 Heat oil for shallow frying in a frying pan and fry the fish in batches until golden and almost cooked. Transfer the fried fish to a large ovenproof dish and keep warm while you prepare the other ingredients.

3 Make the sauce in a wok or large pan. Fry the ginger, garlic and onion in the oil for 5 minutes or until the onion is softened but not browned.

4 Add the pepper squares and carrot strips and stir-fry for 1 minute.

5 Put the cornflour in a small bowl and add a little of the water to make a paste. Stir in the remaining water, the vinegar and the sugar. Pour the cornflour mixture over the vegetables in the wok and stir until the sauce boils and thickens a little. Season with fish sauce and salt and pepper if needed.

6 Add the fish to the sauce and reheat without stirring. Transfer to a serving platter and garnish with chilli and spring onions. Serve with plain boiled rice.

COOK'S TIP
Red snapper or small sea bass could be used for this recipe, in which case ask your fishmonger to cut it into fillets.

FISH STEW with VEGETABLES

Sinigang, *as it is known in the Philippines, is a soured soup-like stew, which many Filipinos consider to be their national dish. It is always served with noodles or rice, and seafood — either prawns or thin slivers of fish fillet — is often added for good measure.*

SERVES 4–6

15ml/1 tbsp tamarind pulp or 5ml/1 tsp
   concentrated tamarind pulp
150ml/¼ pint/⅔ cup warm water
2 tomatoes, roughly chopped
115g/4oz spinach or Chinese
   kangkong leaves
115g/4oz peeled, cooked large prawns
   (jumbo shrimp), thawed if frozen
1.2 litres/2 pints/5 cups prepared fish
   stock (see Cook's Tip)
½ mooli (daikon), peeled and
   finely diced
115g/4oz/¾ cup French (green) beans,
   cut into 1cm/½in lengths
225g/8oz piece of cod or haddock fillet,
   skinned and cut into strips
fish sauce, to taste
squeeze of lemon juice, to taste
salt and ground black pepper
plain boiled rice or noodles, to serve

1 Put the tamarind pulp in a large bowl, if using, and pour over the warm water. Set aside. Peel and chop the tomatoes, and discard the seeds. Strip the spinach or kangkong leaves from the stems and tear into small pieces. Set aside.

2 Using your hands, remove the heads and shells from the prawns, if necessary, leaving the tails intact.

3 Pour the prepared fish stock into a large pan and add the finely diced mooli. Cook the mooli for 5 minutes, then add the chopped green beans. Continue to cook the stew gently for 3–5 minutes more.

4 Add the fish strips, tomatoes and spinach or kangkong leaves. Strain in the tamarind juice or add the concentrated tamarind, stir until dissolved, and cook for 2 minutes. Stir in the prawns and cook for 1–2 minutes to heat through.

5 Season the stew with salt and freshly ground black pepper, and add a little fish sauce and lemon juice to taste. Transfer the stew to individual warmed serving bowls, and serve with either plain boiled rice or noodles.

COOK'S TIP
A good fish stock is essential for Sinigang. Ask your fishmonger for about 675g/1½lb fish bones. Wash them, then place in a pan with 2 litres/3½ pints/8 cups water. Add half a peeled onion, a 2.5cm/1in piece of bruised fresh root ginger, and a little salt and pepper. Bring to the boil, skim, then simmer for 20 minutes. Cool slightly, then strain. Freeze any unused stock.

RICE AND NOODLES

The unassertive flavours of rice and noodles make them perfect partners

for the fragrant, aromatic foods of South-east Asia. Rice grows in

abundance throughout the region. Like noodles, it is a staple food, and

is eaten with every meal on a daily basis.

FESTIVE RICE

Rice is the staple food throughout South-east Asia. There are numerous varieties, but the two commonly used ones are polished white long grain and glutinous rice. Generally, any long grain rice will produce good results, but Thai fragrant rice is particularly delicious.

SERVES 8

450g/1lb/2⅓ cups Thai fragrant rice
   or other long grain rice
60ml/4 tbsp vegetable oil
2 garlic cloves, crushed
2 onions, finely sliced
5cm/2in piece fresh turmeric, crushed
750ml/1¼ pints/3 cups water
400g/14oz can coconut milk
1–2 lemon grass stalks, bruised
1–2 pandan (screwpine) leaves
   (optional)
salt

For the accompaniments
omelette strips
2 fresh red chillies, shredded
cucumber chunks
tomato wedges
Deep-fried Onions
Coconut and Peanut Relish
prawn (shrimp) crackers

1 Wash the rice thoroughly in several changes of water. Drain well.

2 Heat the vegetable oil in a wok or frying pan and gently fry the crushed garlic, finely sliced onions and crushed fresh turmeric for a few minutes until soft but not browned.

3 Add the rice and stir well so that each grain is coated in oil, and the rice mixes with the garlic, onion and turmeric. Pour in the water and coconut milk and add the bruised lemon grass, pandan leaves, if using, and add salt to taste.

4 Bring to the boil, stirring well. Cover the pan and cook gently for about 15–20 minutes, until all of the liquid has been absorbed.

5 Remove the pan from the heat. Cover with a clean dishtowel, put on the lid and leave the pan to stand in a warm place for 15 minutes. Remove the lemon grass and pandan leaves, if used.

6 Turn out the rice on to a warmed serving platter and garnish with the accompaniments before serving.

COOK'S TIP
It is the custom to shape the rice into a cone (to represent a volcano) and then surround it with the accompaniments. Shape the rice with oiled hands or use a conical sieve.

COCONUT RICE

This is a very popular way of cooking rice throughout the whole of South-east Asia. Nasi uduk, as it is known in Indonesia, makes a wonderful accompaniment to any meat dish, and goes particularly well with fish, chicken and pork.

SERVES 4–6

350g/12oz Thai fragrant rice
400g/14oz can coconut milk
300ml/½ pint/1¼ cups water
2.5ml/½ tsp ground coriander
2.5cm/1in piece cinnamon stick
1 lemon grass stalk, bruised
1 pandan (screwpine) or bay leaf or
   2–3 drops screwpine essence
salt
fresh coriander (cilantro) sprigs and
   Deep-fried Onions, to garnish

1 Wash the rice in several changes of water and then put in a large pan with the coconut milk, water, coriander, cinnamon stick, lemon grass and pandan, bay leaf or screwpine essence, if using, and salt. Bring to the boil, stirring constantly to prevent the rice from settling on the base of the pan. Cover with a lid and cook over a very low heat for 12–15 minutes, or until the coconut milk has been absorbed.

2 Fork through and remove the lemon grass, cinnamon, and pandan or bay leaf. Cover and cook for 3 minutes more.

3 Cover the pan with a tight-fitting lid and continue to cook over the lowest possible heat for 3–5 minutes more.

4 When the rice is ready, pile on to a warm serving dish and garnish with the coriander sprigs and crisp Deep-fried Onions. Serve immediately.

COOK'S TIP
If you wish to use fresh coconut milk, crack open the coconut and remove the clear water (this makes an excellent cooling drink). Using a small, sharp knife, remove the flesh in sections, then peel off the brown skin. Process the flesh in a food processor, and squeeze out the milk through a muslin (cheesecloth) cloth.

MALACCA FRIED RICE

Using leftover rice to make up a new dish is a common practice all over the East. In most Eastern countries, rice is equivalent to wealth and it is never thrown away. It is believed that if you throw away wealth it will never return to you.

SERVES 4–6

2 eggs
45ml/3 tbsp vegetable oil
4 shallots or 1 onion, finely chopped
5ml/1 tsp grated fresh root ginger
1 garlic clove, crushed
225g/8oz peeled prawn (shrimp) tails,
　raw or cooked
5–10ml/1–2 tsp chilli sauce (optional)
3 spring onions (scallions), green part
　only, roughly chopped
225g/8oz/2 cups frozen peas, thawed
225g/8oz thickly sliced roast pork, diced
45ml/3 tbsp light soy sauce
350g/12oz long grain rice, cooked and
　allowed to become completely cold
salt and ground black pepper

1 In a bowl, beat the eggs well, and season to taste with salt and ground black pepper.

2 Heat 15ml/1 tbsp of the vegetable oil in a wok or large pan, pour in the eggs and allow them to set, without stirring, for less than a minute.

3 Roll up the pancake with your hands, then cut it into thin strips and set aside. The pancake can be allowed to cool down to room temperature, although it can also be served hot, if you like.

COOK'S TIP
Store cooked, cooled rice in an airtight container in the refrigerator. Heat the rice thoroughly, and make sure the grains are piping hot when using precooked and cooled rice in any recipe.

4 Heat the remaining vegetable oil in the wok, add the shallots or onions, chopped ginger, garlic and prawn tails and cook gently for 1–2 minutes. Keep stirring the contents of the wok to ensure that the garlic doesn't burn.

5 Add the chilli sauce, if using, spring onions, peas, pork and soy sauce. Stir to heat through, then add the rice. Fry the rice over a moderate heat for 6–8 minutes. Turn into a warmed serving dish and decorate with the pancake.

INDONESIAN FRIED RICE

One of the most familiar and well-known Indonesian dishes, Nasi Goreng is a marvellous way to use up leftover rice, chicken and meats such as pork. It is important that the rice is quite cold and the grains are separate before adding the other ingredients.

SERVES 4–6

350g/12oz/¾ cups dry weight long grain
   rice, such as basmati, cooked and
   allowed to become completely cold
2 eggs
30ml/2 tbsp water
105ml/7 tbsp vegetable oil
225g/8oz pork fillet or fillet of beef
115g/4oz peeled, cooked prawns (shrimp)
175–225g/6–8oz cooked chicken, chopped
2–3 fresh red chillies, seeded and sliced
1cm/½in cube shrimp paste
2 garlic cloves, crushed
1 onion, sliced
30ml/2 tbsp dark soy sauce or
   45–60ml/3–4 tbsp tomato ketchup
salt and ground black pepper
celery leaves, fresh coriander (cilantro)
   sprigs, to garnish

1 Once the rice is cooked and cooled, fork it through to separate the grains and keep it in a covered pan or dish until required.

2 Beat the eggs with seasoning and the water and make two or three omelettes in a frying pan, with a minimum of oil. Roll up each omelette and cut into strips when cold. Set aside.

3 Cut the pork or beef into neat strips and put the meat, prawns and chicken pieces in separate bowls. Shred one of the chillies and reserve it.

COOK'S TIP
Always store cooked and cooled rice in the refrigerator.

4 Put the shrimp paste, with the remaining chilli, garlic and onion, in a food processor and grind to a paste, or pound using a pestle and mortar.

5 Fry the paste in the remaining hot oil, without browning, until it gives off a rich, spicy aroma. Add the strips of pork or beef and fry over a high heat to seal in the juices. Stir constantly to prevent the meat sticking to the bottom of the pan.

6 Add the prawns, cook for 2 minutes and then stir in the chicken, cold rice, dark soy sauce or ketchup and seasoning to taste. Stir constantly to keep the rice light and fluffy and prevent it from sticking to the base of the pan.

7 Turn on to a hot platter and garnish with the omelette strips, celery leaves, reserved shredded fresh chilli and coriander sprigs.

PINEAPPLE FRIED RICE

When buying a pineapple, look for a sweet-smelling fruit with an even brownish/yellow skin. To test for ripeness, tap the base – a dull sound indicates that the fruit is ripe. The flesh should also give slightly when pressed.

SERVES 4–6

1 pineapple
30ml/2 tbsp vegetable oil
1 small onion, finely chopped
2 fresh green chillies, seeded and chopped
225g/8oz lean pork, cut into strips
115g/4oz cooked, peeled prawns (shrimp)
675–900g/1½–2lb/3–4 cups plain boiled
   rice, cooked and completely cold
50g/2oz/⅓ cup roasted cashew nuts
2 spring onions (scallions), chopped
30ml/2 tbsp fish sauce
15ml/1 tbsp soy sauce
2 fresh red chillies, sliced, and 10–12 fresh
   mint leaves (optional), to garnish

1 Using a sharp knife, cut the pineapple into quarters. Remove the flesh from both halves by cutting around inside the skin. Reserve the pineapple skin shells for serving the rice.

2 Slice the pineapple flesh and chop it into small even-size cubes. You will need about 115g/4oz of pineapple in total. Any remaining fruit can be reserved for use in a dessert.

3 Heat the oil in a wok or large pan. Add the onion and chillies and fry for about 3–5 minutes until softened. Add the strips of pork and cook until they have browned on all sides.

4 Stir in the prawns and rice and toss well together. Continue to stir-fry until the rice is thoroughly heated.

5 Add the chopped pineapple, cashew nuts and spring onions. Season to taste with fish sauce and soy sauce.

6 Spoon into the pineapple skin shells. Garnish with sliced red chillies, and with shredded mint leaves, if you like.

COOK'S TIP
This dish is ideal to prepare for a special occasion meal. Served in the pineapple skin shells, it is sure to be the talking point of the dinner.

THAI FRIED NOODLES

Phat Thai, as this dish is known, has a fascinating flavour and texture. It is made with rice noodles, combined with shellfish and beancurd, a range of vegetables and ground peanuts, and is considered one of the national dishes of Thailand.

SERVES 4–6

350g/12oz rice noodles
45ml/3 tbsp vegetable oil
15ml/1 tbsp chopped garlic
16 raw king prawns (jumbo shrimp),
    peeled, tails left intact and deveined
2 eggs, lightly beaten
15ml/1 tbsp dried shrimps, rinsed
30ml/2 tbsp pickled white radish
50g/2oz fried beancurd or tofu, chopped
2.5ml/½ tsp dried chilli flakes
115g/4oz garlic chives, cut into 5cm/
    2in lengths
225g/8oz/1 cup beansprouts
50g/2oz/⅓ cup roasted peanuts,
    coarsely ground
5ml/1 tsp granulated sugar
15ml/1 tbsp dark soy sauce
30ml/2 tbsp fish sauce
30ml/2 tbsp tamarind juice or 5ml/1 tsp
    concentrated tamarind pulp
30ml/2 tbsp fresh coriander (cilantro)
    leaves and 1 kaffir lime, to garnish

1 Soak the noodles in a bowl of warm water for 20–30 minutes, then drain.

2 Heat 15ml/1 tbsp of the oil in a wok or large pan. Add the garlic and fry until golden. Stir in the prawns and cook for 1–2 minutes until pink, tossing from time to time. Remove and set aside.

3 Heat another 15ml/1 tbsp of oil in the pan. Add the eggs and tilt the wok to spread them into a thin sheet. Stir to scramble and break the egg into small pieces. Remove from the pan and set aside with the prawns.

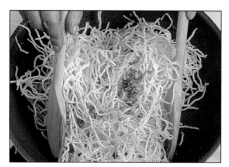

4 Heat the remaining oil in the same pan. Add the dried shrimps, pickled radish, beancurd or tofu and dried chillies. Stir-fry briefly. Add the soaked noodles and stir-fry for 5 minutes.

5 Add the garlic chives, half the beansprouts and half the peanuts. Season with the granulated sugar, soy sauce, fish sauce and tamarind juice or pulp. Mix well and cook until the noodles are completely heated through.

6 Return the prawn and egg mixture to the pan and mix with the noodles. Serve garnished with the rest of the beansprouts, peanuts, coriander leaves and kaffir lime wedges, if using.

COOK'S TIP
Pickled white radish is available in jars from Asian food stores and markets.

MIXED MEAT FRIED NOODLES with PRAWNS

This fried noodle dish, known as bamie goreng, *is wonderfully accommodating. To the basic recipe you can add other vegetables, such as mushrooms, tiny pieces of chayote, broccoli, leeks or beansprouts. As with fried rice, you can use whatever you have to hand.*

SERVES 6–8

450g/1lb dried egg noodles
115g/4oz chicken breast fillets, skinned
115g/4oz pork fillet
115g/4oz calf's liver (optional)
2 eggs, beaten
90ml/6 tbsp vegetable oil
25g/1oz butter or margarine
2 garlic cloves, crushed
115g/4oz peeled, cooked prawns
    (shrimp)
115g/4oz spinach or Chinese leaves
    (Chinese cabbage)
2 celery sticks, finely sliced
4 spring onions (scallions), shredded
about 60ml/4 tbsp chicken stock
dark soy sauce and light soy sauce
salt and ground black pepper
Deep-fried Onions and celery leaves,
    to garnish (optional)

1 Cook the noodles in salted, boiling water for 3–4 minutes. Drain, rinse with cold water and drain again. Set aside until required.

2 Finely slice the chicken, pork fillet and calf's liver, if using.

3 Season the eggs. Heat 5ml/1 tsp oil with the butter or margarine in a small pan until melted and then stir in the eggs and keep stirring until scrambled. Set them aside.

4 Heat the remaining oil in a wok or large pan and fry the garlic with the chicken, pork and liver, if using, for 2–3 minutes, until they change colour. Add the prawns, spinach or Chinese leaves, celery and spring onions, tossing well.

5 Add the cooked, drained noodles and toss well again so that all the ingredients are well mixed. Add enough stock just to moisten, and dark and light soy sauce to taste. Stir in the beaten eggs. Garnish the dish with Deep-fried Onions and celery leaves.

COOK'S TIP

When choosing ingredients for this dish, bear in mind the need to achieve a balance of colour, flavour and texture.

CRISPY FRIED RICE VERMICELLI

Mee krob *is usually served at celebration meals. It is a crisp tangle of fried rice vermicelli, with minced pork, prawns, dried shrimp and beansprouts, tossed in a piquant sweet-and-sour sauce and garnished with strips of omelette.*

SERVES 4–6

vegetable oil, for frying
175g/6oz rice vermicelli
15ml/1 tbsp chopped garlic
4–6 dried chillies, seeded and chopped
30ml/2 tbsp chopped shallot
15ml/1 tbsp dried shrimps, rinsed
115g/4oz minced (ground) pork
115g/4oz peeled, raw prawns (shrimp), chopped
30ml/2 tbsp brown bean sauce
30ml/2 tbsp rice wine vinegar
45ml/3 tbsp fish sauce
75g/3oz palm sugar or light brown sugar
30ml/2 tbsp tamarind or lime juice
115g/4oz/½ cup beansprouts
salt and ground black pepper

For the garnish
2 spring onions (scallions), shredded
30ml/2 tbsp fresh coriander (cilantro) sprigs
2 heads pickled garlic (optional)
2-egg omelette, rolled and sliced
2 fresh red chillies, chopped

1 Heat the oil in a wok or large pan. Cut the vermicelli into handfuls about 7.5cm/3in long, and deep-fry until they puff up. Remove. Drain on kitchen paper.

2 Leave 30ml/2 tbsp of the hot oil in the pan. Add the garlic, chillies, shallot and shrimps and fry for 2–3 minutes.

3 Add the pork and stir-fry for about 3–4 minutes, until it is no longer pink. Add the prawns and fry for 2 minutes. Remove the mixture and set aside.

4 To the same pan, add the brown bean sauce, vinegar, fish sauce and palm sugar or brown sugar. Bring to a gentle boil, stir to dissolve the sugar and cook until thick and syrupy.

5 Add the tamarind or lime juice and adjust the seasoning. It should be sweet, sour and salty.

6 Reduce the heat. Add the pork and prawn mixture and the beansprouts to the sauce; stir to mix.

7 Add the rice noodles and toss gently to coat them with the sauce. Transfer the noodles to a platter. Garnish with spring onions, coriander leaves, pickled garlic, omelette strips and red chillies.

COURGETTES with NOODLES

Any vegetable from the same family as courgette or squash can be used in this Indonesian recipe, which is known as oseng oseng. It is very similar to a dish enjoyed in Malaysia, and there are strong links between the cuisines of these two neighbouring countries.

SERVES 4–6

450g/1lb courgettes (zucchini)
1 onion, finely sliced
1 garlic clove, finely chopped
30ml/2 tbsp vegetable oil
2.5ml/½ tsp ground turmeric
2 tomatoes, chopped
45ml/3 tbsp water
115g/4oz peeled, cooked prawns (shrimp)
25g/1oz cellophane noodles
salt

COOK'S TIP
Keep an eye on the time as cellophane noodles soften very quickly.

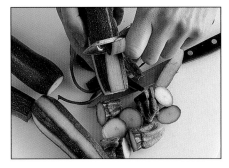

1 Use a potato peeler to cut thin strips from the outside of each courgette. Cut the courgettes into neat slices, then set aside. Fry the onion and garlic in hot oil in a pan; do not allow to brown.

2 Add the turmeric, courgette slices, chopped tomatoes, water and the cooked prawns.

3 Put the noodles in a large pan and pour over enough boiling water to cover. Leave the noodles to soak for a minute and then drain. Cut the noodles into 5cm/2in lengths and then add them to the vegetables.

4 Cover the pan with a lid and allow everything to cook in its own steam for 2–3 minutes. Toss well together. Season the noodles with salt to taste, and transfer to a warmed serving bowl.

NOODLES with CHICKEN, PRAWNS and HAM

*The cuisine of the Philippines is a harmonious blend of Malay, Chinese and Spanish
influences. This recipe has Chinese origins, and is known in Malaysia as* pansit guisado.
Any kind of meat can be cooked with the prawns.

SERVES 4–6

285g/10oz dried egg noodles
15ml/1 tbsp vegetable oil
1 onion, chopped
1 garlic clove, crushed
2.5cm/1 in piece fresh root ginger, grated
50g/2oz canned water chestnuts, drained
   and sliced
15ml/1 tbsp light soy sauce
30ml/2 tbsp fish sauce or chicken stock
175g/6oz cooked chicken breast, sliced
150g/5oz cooked ham, thickly sliced, cut
   into short fingers
225g/8oz peeled, cooked prawn
   (shrimp) tails
175g/6oz/¾ cup beansprouts
200g/7oz canned baby corn, drained
2 limes, cut into wedges, and 1 small
   bunch fresh coriander (cilantro),
   shredded, to garnish

1 Soak the egg noodles in a large bowl of water, and cook them according to the instructions on the packet. Drain the noodles and set aside.

2 Meanwhile, in a wok or large pan, fry the onion, garlic and ginger until soft. Add the water chestnuts, soy sauce and fish sauce or chicken stock, and the chicken and ham and prawn tails.

3 Add the noodles, beansprouts and corn. Stir-fry for 6–8 minutes. Garnish with the lime wedges and shredded coriander. Serve immediately.

COOK'S TIP
Egg noodles can be prepared in advance. Cook them up to 24 hours before they are needed, and keep them in a large bowl of cold water.

GLOSSARY

Almonds Available whole, flaked (slivered) and ground, these sweet nuts impart a sumptuous richness to curries.

Aubergines Numerous aubergine varieties exist in Asia, where the vegetable has been grown for more than 2,000 years. Aubergine absorbs the flavours of other ingredients, and benefits from being cooked with strongly flavoured foods and seasonings.

Banana leaves Traditionally made into small parcels to steam foods, banana leaves are sold in Asian food stores. Squares of lightly oiled kitchen foil may be used instead.

Bangkuang (yambean) A major vegetable crop in South-east Asia, bangkuang, or yambean, is peeled and cut into strips before use in stir-fries, spring rolls and salads.

Basil One of the oldest herbs known to man, basil is thought to have originated in India, although it is more widely used in Asia, in Laos, Cambodia, Vietnam and in Thailand, where a variety known as Thai basil is grown. Add basil to curries and salads.

Beancurd Fresh beancurd is commonly known by its Japanese name, tofu. Made from soya beans, it is a source of protein in vegetarian diets. It can be cooked in almost any way with a vast number of ingredients, sweet and savoury. Yellow beancurd is usually only available from Asian food stores.

Chillies All varieties of chilli are native to tropical America, and were introduced to Asia by European traders after Christopher Columbus took them home to Spain. Fresh and dried chillies are used to add heat and flavour to sauces, sambals and salads, and are added to cooked dishes, such as stocks, soups, curries, stir-fries, and braised dishes.

Coconut milk This is available canned or it can be made at home from desiccated (dry, unsweetened, shredded) coconut.

Coriander Fresh coriander is a favourite ingredient in all Asian countries, and its unique delicate flavour and bright green colour makes it a popular garnish for curries. It is also available ground and dried.

Creamed coconut Coconut cream left to solidify and moulded into blocks is used to add richness to savoury and sweet dishes. A small quantity can be cut off the block and stirred into a dish just before serving, or it can be diluted with boiling water to produce coconut milk.

Curry pastes Wet blends of spices, herbs and chillies that are used as the basis of a curry. Different spice blends will produce different flavours. As they contain fresh ingredients, curry pastes need to be refrigerated and used as required.

Curry powder These are dry blends of spices and chillies. Different blends and roasting times of the spices and chillies produce different flavoured powders.

Fish sauce This is a seasoning for savoury dishes in Thai and Vietnamese cooking, and is also used to make dipping sauces. In Vietnam, it is made using shrimps, but in Thailand, the sauce is more often made using salted, fermented fish.

Kaffir limes This fruit is not a true lime, but belongs to a subspecies of the citrus family. Native to South-east Asia, kaffir limes have dark green knobbly skins. The fruit is not edible, and although the rind can be used in cooking, it is the fragrant leaves that are the most prized. Kaffir limes are synonymous with Thai cooking, and are also used in Indonesia, Malaysia, Burma and Vietnam. The leaves are torn or shredded.

Galangal A flavouring agent widely used in South-east Asian shellfish and meat dishes. Galangal is pounded with shallots, garlic and chillies to make a spice paste for curries and dipping sauces. It also can be sliced for use in soups and dressings.

Garlic A standard ingredient in most South-east Asian curries, garlic is used crushed, chopped or as whole cloves.

Ginger Fresh root ginger is a key ingredient in South-east Asian cooking. Ground ginger is a useful standby but it lacks the flavour of the fresh spice.

Lemon grass This long, citrus-flavoured bulb is a distinctive ingredient in South-east Asian cooking, especially in Thailand, Malaysia and Indonesia. Whole bulbs can be bruised and added to soups, stews and curries, while the stem can be sliced or chopped for use in stir-fries or salads.

Lentils Small, round dry seeds that should be shelled and cooked before use. Lentils are indigenous to Asia, and are a staple food in many countries.

Mung beans Small, round olive-green beans with a delicate, sweetish flavour. Beansprouts are sprouted mung beans.

Noodles Noodles are eaten on a daily basis throughout South-east Asia. Many noodle varieties are available, which can be made from wheat flour, with or without eggs, or from rice and other starches. Cellophane noodles are made from the starch of mung beans. Noodles are sold fresh and dried.

Sambals South-east Asian sambals are hot, spicy relishes or sauces that have chillies as their key ingredients. They are served in small bowls, and pieces of cooked meat, fish or vegetables are then dipped into the bowl.

Shrimp paste An essential ingredient in curries, rice dishes, satay sauces, dipping sauces, dressings, and braised dishes. Shrimp paste is made from tiny shrimps that have been salted, dried, pounded, and left to ferment in hot and humid conditions.

Tamarind Dried black tamarind pods are sour and sticky. Tamarind is used for its flavour, which is refreshingly tart, without being bitter. Lemon juice may be used a substitute but the flavour will not compare.

Turmeric This bright yellow, bitter-tasting spice is sold ground and fresh, with fresh turmeric being peeled and then grated or sliced in the same way as fresh root ginger. Turmeric is often used as an alternative to saffron, and is used for its colour, as well as for its peppery aroma and warm, musky flavour. Ground turmeric is a key ingredient in curry powders, and is responsible for the characteristic yellow colour.

INDEX

PICTURE CREDITS
Additional picture material
supplied by Life File:
page 11 top right, page 12,
page 13 top and bottom,
page 14, page 15 top
and bottom.